KYUUTO!
JAPANESE CRAFT
AMIGURUMI

D1460765

CHRONICL
SAN FRAN

First published in Japan as *Takamori Tomoko no Ande ne Amigurumi* in 2006 by SHUFU-TO-SEIKATSUSHA.
Copyright © 2006 by Tomoko Takamori and SHUFU-TO-SEI-KATSUSHA.

First published in the United States in 2007 by Chronicle Books LLC.

English translation rights arranged with SHUFU-TO-SEIKAT-SUSHA, Tokyo, through Timo Associates, Inc., Tokyo.

Library of Congress Cataloging-in-Publication Data available.

ISBN: 978-0-8118-6082-6

Manufactured in China

Book design: Satomi Nakata, Andrew Pothecary
(forbiddencolour), Eiko Nishida (cooltiger)
Cover design: River Jukes-Hudson
Photography: Miwa Kumon
Artwork: Tomoko Takamori, Emi Yoshida
Text: Tomoko Takamori
Template drawings: Kayo Sotokawa, Chiaki Sakagawa,
Natsu Kawabe
English copyediting: Alma Reyes Umemoto, Seishi Maruyama
Editor: Tokomo Fujii
Production assistant: Aki Ueda (ricorico)
Chief editor and production: Rico Komanoya (ricorico)

10 9 8 7 6 5 4 3 2

Chronicle Books LLC
680 Second Street
San Francisco, California 94107

www.chroniclebooks.com

Contents

Yarns and Materials Used in This Book

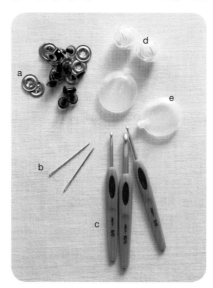

Yarns

Yarns are classified into different types: fine, light, medium, heavy, bulky, and extra-bulky, from the thinnest to the thickest. The right crochet hook needs to be used according to the thickness of the yarn. There are also several types of yarn materials, such as wool, cotton, mohair, nylon, and polyester mixture, so you can enjoy a wide variety of textures, from lustrous to smooth. You can create a unique finish by using unusual types of yarns, such as fur, loop yarn, or napping yarn. If you cannot find some of the yarns used in this book, you may use similar threads or choose from your favorite yarns to improvise your own crochet pattern.

a. Eyes

Eyes come in pairs and in two types: one type is pinned onto the fabric with washers, and the other type is glued directly onto the face of the doll.

b. Tapestry needle

The tip of a tapestry needle is rounded. This type of needle is used for stitching or sewing together several parts of amigurumi, either with an overcast stitch or a whipstitch.

c. Crochet hook

Crochet hooks vary from the thinnest, size #0 (2 mm), to the thickest, size #10 (6 mm). Seven sizes of crochet hooks are used in this book: sizes #1 (2.2 mm and 2.5 mm), #2 (3 mm), #4 (3.5 mm), #6 (4 mm), #8 (5 mm), and #10 (6 mm).

d. Bell

A bell is inserted inside the head so that your amigurumi doll produces a nice sound when you shake it.

e. Squeaker

A squeaker is inserted (with cotton) inside the body of the doll so that the belly makes a cute, squeaky sound when you push it.

Cotton and Embroidery Thread

Synthetic cotton used for handicrafts is stuffed inside the head, body, and other body parts. Embroidery thread is used to sew the mouth.

Materials

HOW TO MAKE THE FACE

The doll's facial expressions change completely depending on the placement of the eyes, nose, and mouth. Check as you position these parts to make sure the face is appealing.

How to Attach the Eyes

Washer

First, stuff some cotton inside the head, and pin all the parts of the face temporarily (eyes, nose, and ears), to determine their approximate positions. Then, take the cotton out of the head and attach the eyes. Pierce the eyes through the fabric from the right side and attach a washer to the wrong side. If the eyes are to be glued, apply glue to the wrong side of the eyes and attach them to the face.

Chain Stitch

Make a foundation chain or a ring to start the pattern. Then, as you work, refer to the Crochet Chart Symbols on page 5. To make the mouth, take 2 or 3 strands of embroidery thread and make a chain stitch.

Whipstitch

Felt is used for creating the nose tip, mouth, and tongue. Cut a piece of felt (without seam allowance) and attach it using fine whipstitches with 2 strands of embroidery thread.

Crochet Chart Symbols

The crochet chart symbols that appear in this book are easy to master.
Please refer to them when making your amigurumi.

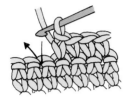 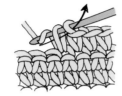

Single Crochet (Make one stitch into one loop.)

 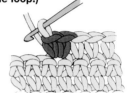

Single Crochet Increase (Make two stitches of single crochet into one loop.)

Single Crochet Decrease (Make one single crochet stitch into two loops.)

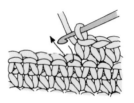 

End Point (slip stitch)

Diagrams show the wrong side of the rows for flat crochet

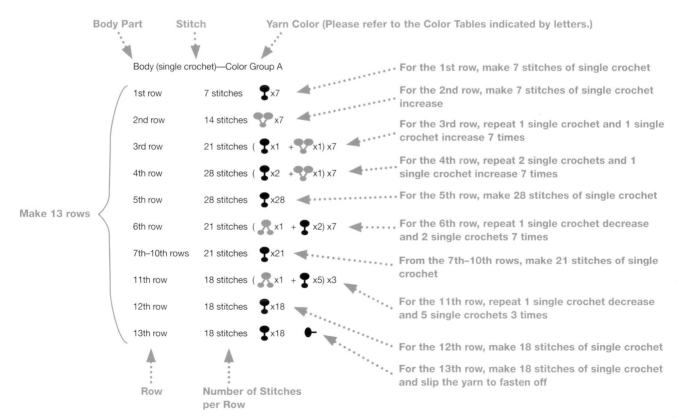

Body Part · · · · Stitch · · · · Yarn Color (Please refer to the Color Tables indicated by letters.)

Body (single crochet)—Color Group A

Row	Stitch	
1st row	7 stitches	x7
2nd row	14 stitches	x7
3rd row	21 stitches	(x1 + x1) x7
4th row	28 stitches	(x2 + x1) x7
5th row	28 stitches	x28
6th row	21 stitches	(x1 + x2) x7
7th–10th rows	21 stitches	x21
11th row	18 stitches	(x1 + x5) x3
12th row	18 stitches	x18
13th row	18 stitches	x18

Make 13 rows

Row · · · · Number of Stitches per Row

For the 1st row, make 7 stitches of single crochet

For the 2nd row, make 7 stitches of single crochet increase

For the 3rd row, repeat 1 single crochet and 1 single crochet increase 7 times

For the 4th row, repeat 2 single crochets and 1 single crochet increase 7 times

For the 5th row, make 28 stitches of single crochet

For the 6th row, repeat 1 single crochet decrease and 2 single crochets 7 times

From the 7th–10th rows, make 21 stitches of single crochet

For the 11th row, repeat 1 single crochet decrease and 5 single crochets 3 times

For the 12th row, make 18 stitches of single crochet

For the 13th row, make 18 stitches of single crochet and slip the yarn to fasten off

5

Let's Begin!

BASIC CROCHET LESSON
Crochet Little Bears with Tomoko!

Even those who have never tried crocheting should find it easy to follow my instructions. Just work in circles with a single crochet, and that's it! Now, let's crochet little bears together.

1 Preparing the Tools

First, let's gather our materials (see page 4). I usually draw an image of the amigurumi I would like to make, and then choose the yarns that fit the image.

2 Crocheting

Choose a crochet hook according to the size of the yarn, then you can start crocheting from the head of the bear. Work in spirals with a single crochet (see page 50). Then, make the body, arms, legs, ears, and nose. If you crochet tightly, the doll will be firm; if you stitch loosely, it will be soft.

3 Checking the Total Balance

When you have finished all the parts, place them on a table and see if they appear close to your image; then check if they are well proportioned as one piece.

4 Stuffing Cotton and Attaching the Eyes

Stuff cotton into the head, body, arms, and legs. The arms and legs are stuffed only around the tips. The finished doll may look different depending on how much cotton you stuff with, so adjust the bulk of the cotton as you like. Then, use washers or glue to attach the eyes.

5 Attaching the Mouth to the Nose

Cut some felt to make the tip of the nose. Make the mouth using a chain stitch with embroidery thread, then sew the parts together using a whipstitch.

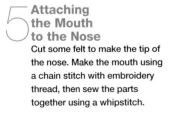

Some of these steps may differ just a little from the instructions presented in the sections, "Assembling the Body Parts," of this book. These are my personal instructions, to help you get started with your very own amigurumi.

6 Confirming the Total Balance Again

Tack all the stuffed parts together with marking pins, and check the entire proportion again. If you find something wrong, adjust the stuffed cotton.

7 Sewing All the Parts Together

First, sew the head onto the body using an overcast stitch (picking up each chain of the last row in the head and body with a tapestry needle). If you are using different colors for the head and body, use the head's color. Then, sew the arms and legs onto the body using an overcast stitch.

Finalizing the Doll

Look at the picture of your drawn image and the finished bear. How is it? Don't you think it's cute? You can change the colors or use a different size yarn to make your own stuffed little bear.

Making the Face

Sew on the ears and nose using an overcast stitch. Fold the ears in half into a semicircular shape, and sew them bending the insides slightly. The stuffed bear is finished!

Little Teddy Bear

Let's go somewhere with a couple of these little teddy bears in your bag!

Striped Teddy Bear

This striped teddy bear's name is Puru.

Big Teddy Bear

If you hug him, he will squeak.

Jackrabbit

A jackrabbit in pink will make you think!

Citron Puppy

What could he be thinking about?
That's a secret.

Fluffy Animals

They look fluffy and feel fluffier.

Butterflies

It's always like spring!

Cotton Puppies

We are made of 100% cotton and
love the warm days.
We look cool in the afternoon sun,
don't you think?

Black and White Kittens

Is it a black kitten wearing white socks?
Or maybe a white kitten wearing a black suit?

Frogs on
a Holiday

Little frogs can be so many different colors! Tree frog, green frog, wrinkled frog—one takes shelter from the rain, one takes a nap, and another gazes away...

Little Duckling

Life can be tough for us little ducklings, but I'm trying my best!

Sheep from Woolen Planet

We live in the Woolen Planet's garden of princes.
Now, we've come to visit the planet Earth.

Cotton Candy Elephants

We look like fluffy cotton candies,
but don't bite us because we may not be tasty!

American Lions

We love to dress up! It's a lot of fun!

Piggies in Love

We cuddle each other here and there ...
Don't disturb our little world.

Cat-like Tiger

I may look like a kitten, but I'm a little cub.
When I grow up, I'm going to be strong like Dad (or Mom?)!

Colorful
Donkeys

Let's dance in a world full of mirror balls, soda water, and bubbles bursting everywhere!

Boy and Girl

Our matching berets
look cool, don't they?

White Seal

Thanks for the scarf, Mom!

Pattern Methods

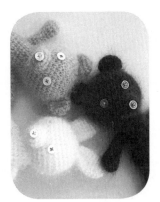

● Little Teddy Bear

See pages 10–11 for photos.

Yarns

Medium type

Doll #1: Brick red, 0.7 oz (20 g); Plain,
0.2 oz (5 g)

Doll #2: Blue, 0.7 oz (20 g); Golden yellow,
0.2 oz (5 g)

Doll #3: Plain, 0.7 oz (20 g); Light brown,
0.2 oz (5 g)

Doll #4: Wasabi green, 0.7 oz (20 g); Pale
blue, 0.2 oz (5 g)

Doll #5: Golden yellow, 0.7 oz (20 g); Pale
blue, 0.2 oz (5 g)

Tools

Size 1 (2.5 mm) crochet hook
Tapestry needle

Other materials

5 pairs of washer beads for 0.2 in (0.6 cm)
eyes: orange for doll #1, yellow for dolls
#2 and #3, blue for dolls #4 and #5
Small piece of black felt
Black embroidery thread
Synthetic cotton, 0.4 oz (10 g)

Tips

Pick up a single strand of yarn, and start
from a foundation ring with only single
crochet stitches. Leave a long tail at the
end and fasten off. Stuff cotton into every
body part except for the ears and nose.
Use overcast stitches to attach the ears,
nose, eyes, head, arms and legs. Sew the
ears and nose onto the head, then attach
the eyes. Sew the head, then the arms
and legs onto the body.

How to Crochet (refer to Color Table)
Head (single crochet)—Color Group A

1st row	7 stitches	♀x7
2nd row	14 stitches	x7
3rd row	21 stitches	(♀x1 + x1) x7
4th row	28 stitches	(♀x2 + x1) x7
5th row	35 stitches	(♀x3 + x1) x7
6th row	42 stitches	(♀x4 + x1) x7
7th–9th rows	42 stitches	♀x42
10th row	35 stitches	(x1 + ♀x4) x7
11th row	28 stitches	(x1 + ♀x3) x7
12th row	21 stitches	(x1 + ♀x2) x7
13th row	18 stitches	(x1 + ♀x5) x3 ●—

How to Crochet
Body (single crochet)—Color Group A

1st row	7 stitches	♀x7
2nd row	14 stitches	x7
3rd row	21 stitches	(♀x1 + x1) x7
4th row	28 stitches	(♀x2 + x1) x7
5th row	28 stitches	♀x28
6th row	21 stitches	(x1 + ♀x2) x7
7th–10th rows	21 stitches	♀x21
11th row	18 stitches	(x1 + ♀x5) x3
12th row	18 stitches	♀x18
13th row	18 stitches	♀x18 ●—

Color Table

	Doll 1	Doll 2	Doll 3	Doll 4	Doll 5
Color Group A (main body)	Brick red	Blue	Plain	Wasabi green	Golden yellow
Color Group B (nose, tips of arms and feet)	Plain	Golden yellow	Light brown	Pale blue	Pale blue

How to Crochet

Arms (single crochet), 2 pieces

			Color Group
1st row	7 stitches	♟x7	B
2nd row	7 stitches	♟x7	B
3rd–8th rows	7 stitches	♟x7 ●━	A

How to Crochet

Legs (single crochet), 2 pieces

			Color Group
1st row	5 stitches	♟x5	B
2nd row	10 stitches	♣x5	B
3rd–8th rows	10 stitches	♟x10 ●━	A

How to Crochet

Ears (single crochet), 2 pieces—Color Group A

1st row	7 stitches	♟x7
2nd row	14 stitches	♣x7 ●━

How to Crochet

Nose (single crochet)—Color Group B

1st row	5 stitches	♟x5
2nd row	10 stitches	♣x5 ●━

Assembling the Body Parts

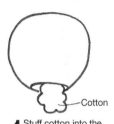

Cotton

1 Stuff cotton into the head.

Cotton

2 Stuff cotton into the body.

Cotton

Do not stuff cotton around the upper parts

3 Stuff cotton into the tips of the arms and into the legs.

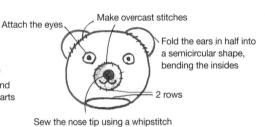

Attach the eyes

Make overcast stitches

Fold the ears in half into a semicircular shape, bending the insides

2 rows

Sew the nose tip using a whipstitch

4 Make the nose tip and mouth, and sew the ears and nose on by flattening the joint sides with overcast stitches, then, attach the eyes.

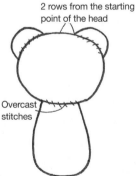

2 rows from the starting point of the head

Overcast stitches

5 Sew the head onto the body with overcast stitches.

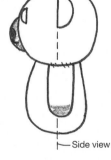

Side view

6 Sew the arms to the seam of the head and the body with overcast stitches, flattening the joint sides.

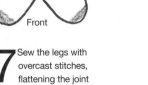

Back

Starting point of the body

3 rows

Front

7 Sew the legs with overcast stitches, flattening the joint sides.

Finished Little Teddy Bear

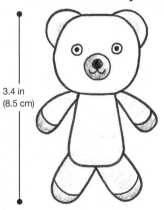

3.4 in (8.5 cm)

Stuff cotton into every body part except for the ears and nose

Actual size of the nose tip and mouth

Black felt

Chain stitches with 2 strands of black embroidery thread

● Striped Teddy Bear

See pages 12–13 for photos.

Yarns

Heavy type

Doll #1: Golden yellow, 1.1 oz (30 g); Blue,
  0.5 oz (15 g); White, 0.7 oz (20 g); Red,
  0.2 oz (5 g)
Doll #2: Orange, 1.1 oz (30 g); Blue,
  0.5 oz (15 g); Light brown, 0.7 oz (20 g);
  Sky blue, 0.2 oz (5 g)
Doll #3: Green, 1.4 oz (40 g);
  Red, 0.5 oz (15 g); Blue, 0.4 oz (10 g);
  White, 0.2 oz (5 g)

Tools

Size 2 (3 mm) crochet hook
Tapestry needle

Other materials

3 pairs of washer beads for 0.6 in
  (1.5 cm) eyes: red for doll #1, yellow for
  doll #2, green for doll #3
Small piece of black felt
Black embroidery thread
Synthetic cotton, 1.8 oz (50 g)
Bell, 1 piece

Tips

Pick up a single strand of yarn, and start
from foundation ring with only single
crochet stitches. Leave a long tail at the
end and fasten off. Stuff cotton into every
body part except for the ears and nose.
Insert a bell in the head and use overcast
stitches to attach the ears, nose, eyes,
head, arms and legs. Sew the ears and
nose onto the head, then attach the eyes.
Sew the head, then the arms and legs
onto the body.

How to Crochet (refer to color table)

Head (single crochet)
Dolls #1, #2—Color Group A; Doll #3—Color Group C

1st row	7 stitches	x7
2nd row	14 stitches	x7
3rd row	21 stitches	(x1 + x1) x7
4th row	28 stitches	(x2 + x1) x7
5th row	35 stitches	(x3 + x1) x7
6th row	42 stitches	(x4 + x1) x7
7th row	49 stitches	(x5 + x1) x7
8th row	56 stitches	(x6 + x1) x7
9th row	63 stitches	(x7 + x1) x7
10th–14th rows	63 stitches	x63
15th row	56 stitches	(x1 + x7) x7
16th row	49 stitches	(x1 + x6) x7
17th row	42 stitches	(x1 + x5) x7
18th row	35 stitches	(x1 + x4) x7
19th row	28 stitches	(x1 + x3) x7
20th row	21 stitches	(x1 + x2) x7

How to Crochet

Body (single crochet)

Row	Stitches	Pattern	Color Group
1st row	7 stitches	x7	D
2nd row	14 stitches	x7	D
3rd row	21 stitches	(x1 + x1) x7	D
4th row	28 stitches	(x2 + x1) x7	D
5th row	35 stitches	(x3 + x1) x7	D
6th row	42 stitches	(x4 + x1) x7	D
7th row	42 stitches	x42	D
8th row	42 stitches	x42	D
9th row	42 stitches	x42	C
10th row	35 stitches	(x1 + x4) x7	C
11th row	35 stitches	x35	B
12th row	35 stitches	x35	C
13th row	35 stitches	x35	C
14th row	35 stitches	x35	B
15th row	35 stitches	x35	C
16th row	28 stitches	(x1 + x3) x7	C
17th row	28 stitches	x28	B
18th row	28 stitches	x28	C
19th row	28 stitches	x28	C
20th row	28 stitches	x28	B
21st row	21 stitches	(x1 + x2) x7	C
22nd row	21 stitches	x21	C

Color Table

	Doll 1	Doll 2	Doll 3
Color Group A (head, tips of arms and feet)	Golden yellow	Orange	White
Color Group B (main body, arms)	Red	Sky blue	Blue
Color Group C (head, main body, arms)	White	Light brown	Green
Color Group D (main body, feet)	Blue	Blue	Red

How to Crochet
Arms (single crochet), 2 pieces

			Color Group
1st row	6 stitches	♀ x6	A
2nd row	12 stitches	♀ x6	A
3rd row	12 stitches	♀ x12	A
4th row	12 stitches	♀ x12	C
5th row	12 stitches	♀ x12	C
6th row	12 stitches	♀ x12	B
7th row	12 stitches	♀ x12	C
8th row	12 stitches	♀ x12	C
9th row	12 stitches	♀ x12	B
10th row	12 stitches	♀ x12	C
11th row	12 stitches	♀ x12	C
12th row	12 stitches	♀ x12	B
13th row	12 stitches	♀ x12	C
14th row	12 stitches	♀ x12	C
15th row	12 stitches	♀ x12	B
16th row	12 stitches	♀ x12 ●━	C

How to Crochet
Legs (single crochet), 2 pieces

			Color Group
1st row	8 stitches	♀ x8	A
2nd row	16 stitches	♀ x8	A
3rd row	16 stitches	♀ x16	A
4th–11th rows	16 stitches	♀ x16 ●━	D

How to Crochet
Ears (single crochet), 2 pieces
Dolls #1, #2—Color Group A
Doll #3—Color Group C

1st row	6 stitches	♀ x6
2nd row	12 stitches	♀ x6
3rd row	18 stitches	(♀ x1 + ♀ x1) x6
4th row	18 stitches	♀ x18 ●━

How to Crochet
Nose (single crochet)
Dolls #1, #2—Color Group C
Doll #3—Color Group A

1st row	7 stitches	♀ x7
2nd row	14 stitches	♀ x14
3rd row	14 stitches	♀ x14 ●━

Assembling the Body Parts (refer to page 51)

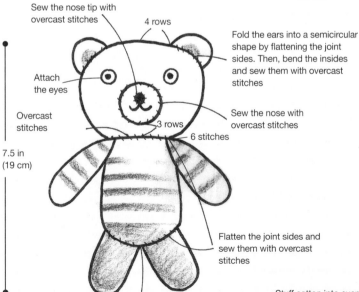

Sew the nose tip with overcast stitches

4 rows

Fold the ears into a semicircular shape by flattening the joint sides. Then, bend the insides and sew them with overcast stitches

Attach the eyes

Overcast stitches

Sew the nose with overcast stitches

3 rows

6 stitches

7.5 in (19 cm)

Flatten the joint sides and sew them with overcast stitches

6 rows from the starting point of the body

Actual size of the nose tip and mouth

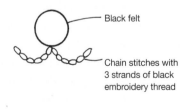

Black felt

Chain stitches with 3 strands of black embroidery thread

Stuff cotton into every body part except for the ears and nose;
Do not stuff cotton around the joint parts of the arms and legs

53

● Big Teddy Bear

See pages 14–15 for photos.

Yarns

Bulky type, 0.5 oz (15 g)
Doll #1: Dark pink
Doll #2: Pale blue
Bulky mixed type, 3.5 oz (100 g)
Doll #1: Mixed pink
Doll #2: Mixed blue

Tools

Size 4 (3.5 mm) crochet hook
Tapestry needle

Other materials

2 pairs of washer beads for 0.4 in
(0.9 cm) eyes: yellow for doll #1,
blue for doll #2
Small piece of black felt
Dark brown embroidery thread
Ribbon, 0.4 in (1 cm) wide
Synthetic cotton, 2.1 oz (60 g)
Bell, 1 piece
Squeaker, 1 piece

Tips

Pick up a single strand of yarn, and start from a foundation ring. Make a rib stitch (refer to facing page) for the head, a single crochet for the body, ears, and nose, and a combination of both stitches for the arms and legs. Leave a long tail at the end and fasten off. Stuff cotton into every body part except for the ears, then insert a bell in the head and a squeaker in the body. Use overcast stitches to attach the ears, nose, eyes, head, arms, and legs. Sew the ears and nose onto the head, then attach the eyes. Sew the head, arms, and legs onto the body. Roll the ribbon around the neck and tie a bow at the back.

How to Crochet (refer to Color Table)

Head (rib stitch)—Color Group A

1st row	7 stitches	×7
2nd row	14 stitches	×7
3rd row	21 stitches	(×1 + ×1) ×7
4th row	28 stitches	(×2 + ×1) ×7
5th row	35 stitches	(×3 + ×1) ×7
6th row	42 stitches	(×4 + ×1) ×7
7th row	49 stitches	(×5 + ×1) ×7
8th row	56 stitches	(×6 + ×1) ×7
9th row	63 stitches	(×7 + ×1) ×7
10th row	70 stitches	(×8 + ×1) ×7
11th–14th rows	70 stitches	×70
15th row	63 stitches	(×1 + ×8) ×7
16th row	56 stitches	(×1 + ×7) ×7
17th row	49 stitches	(×1 + ×6) ×7
18th row	42 stitches	(×1 + ×5) ×7
19th row	35 stitches	(×1 + ×4) ×7
20th row	28 stitches	(×1 + ×3) ×7
21st row	24 stitches	(×1 + ×5) ×4

How to Crochet

Body (single crochet)—Color Group A

1st row	7 stitches	×7
2nd row	14 stitches	×7
3rd row	21 stitches	(×1 + ×1) ×7
4th row	28 stitches	(×2 + ×1) ×7
5th row	35 stitches	(×3 + ×1) ×7
6th–7th rows	35 stitches	×35
8th row	42 stitches	(×4 + ×1) ×7
9th–15th rows	42 stitches	×42
16th row	35 stitches	(×1 + ×4) ×7
17th–20th rows	35 stitches	×35
21th row	28 stitches	(×1 + ×3) ×7
22nd row	28 stitches	×28
23rd row	24 stitches	(×1 + ×5) ×4

Color Table		Doll 1	Doll 2
Color Group A (main body)		Mixed pink	Mixed blue
Color Group B (nose, tips of arms and feet)		Dark pink	Pale blue

How to Crochet

Arms (single crochet, rib stitch), 2 pieces

			Color Group
1st row	6 stitches	x6	B
2nd row	12 stitches	x6	B
3rd row	12 stitches	x12	B
4th–15th rows	12 stitches	x12	A

For arms and legs, do a single crochet from the 1st to the 3rd row, and a rib stitch from the 4th row and onward.

How to Crochet

Legs (single crochet, rib stitch), 2 pieces

			Color Group
1st row	8 stitches	x8	B
2nd row	16 stitches	x8	B
3rd row	16 stitches	x16	B
4th–13th rows	16 stitches	x16	A

How to Crochet

Ears (single crochet)—Color Group A, 2 pieces

1st row	7 stitches	x7
2nd row	14 stitches	x7
3rd row	21 stitches	(x1 + x1) x7
4th row	21 stitches	x21
5th row	21 stitches	x21

How to Crochet

Nose (single crochet)—Color Group B

1st row	6 stitches	x6
2nd row	12 stitches	x6
3rd row	18 stitches	(x1 + x1) x6
4th row	18 stitches	x18
5th row	18 stitches	x18

Assembling the Body Parts (refer to page 51)

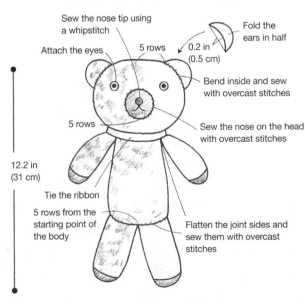

Sew the nose tip using a whipstitch

Attach the eyes

5 rows

Fold the ears in half

0.2 in (0.5 cm)

Bend inside and sew with overcast stitches

Sew the nose on the head with overcast stitches

5 rows

12.2 in (31 cm)

Tie the ribbon

5 rows from the starting point of the body

Flatten the joint sides and sew them with overcast stitches

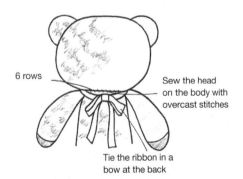

6 rows

Sew the head on the body with overcast stitches

Tie the ribbon in a bow at the back

Stuff cotton into every body part except for the ears and nose; Do not stuff cotton around the joint parts of the arms and legs

Actual size of the nose tip and mouth

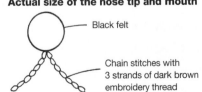

Black felt

Chain stitches with 3 strands of dark brown embroidery thread

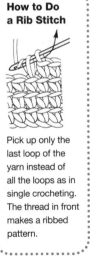

How to Do a Rib Stitch

Pick up only the last loop of the yarn instead of all the loops as in single crocheting. The thread in front makes a ribbed pattern.

● Jackrabbit

See pages 16–17 for photos.

Yarns

Medium type with mohair in mixed fancy
   colors, 0.9 oz (25 g)
Doll #1: Mixed pink
Doll #2: Mixed light brown
Medium type
Doll #1: Pink, 0.9 oz (25 g); Pale blue,
   0.9 oz (25 g); Plain, 0.3 oz (7 g)
Doll #2: Light brown, 1.8 oz (50 g);
   Pink, 0.3 oz (7 g)

Tools

Size 4 (3.5 mm) and 1 (2.5 mm) crochet
   hooks
Tapestry needle

Other materials

2 pairs of pink washer beads for 0.4 in
   (0.9 cm) eyes
Small pieces of black and red felt
Synthetic cotton, 1.8 oz (50 g)
Bell, 1 piece

Tips

Use a size 4 (3.5 mm) crochet hook and
two strands of fancy yarn to knit the tail
and Color Group A parts of the head,
arms, and legs. Work on the ears and the
body with a single strand of medium yarn
and a size 1 (2.5 mm) crochet hook. Stitch
everything with a single crochet from a
foundation ring. Leave a long tail at the
end and fasten off. Stuff cotton into every
body part except for the ears and nose,
then insert a bell inside the head. Use
overcast stitches to attach the ears, nose,
eyes, tongue, arms, legs, and tail. Sew the
ears and nose onto the head, then attach
the eyes and tongue. Sew the head onto
the body. Sew the arms and legs on the
body, then attach the tail at the back.

How to Crochet (refer to Color Table)

Head (single crochet)—Color Group A

1st row	7 stitches	⬥x7
2nd row	14 stitches	⬥x7
3rd row	21 stitches	(⬥x1 + ⬥x1) x7
4th row	28 stitches	(⬥x2 + ⬥x1) x7
5th row	35 stitches	(⬥x3 + ⬥x1) x7
6th row	42 stitches	(⬥x4 + ⬥x1) x7
7th row	49 stitches	(⬥x5 + ⬥x1) x7
8th–11th rows	49 stitches	⬥x49
12th row	42 stitches	(⬥x1 + ⬥x5) x7
13th row	35 stitches	(⬥x1 + ⬥x4) x7
14th row	28 stitches	(⬥x1 + ⬥x3) x7
15th row	21 stitches	(⬥x1 + ⬥x2) x7
16th row	18 stitches	(⬥x1 + ⬥x5) x3 ●—

How to Crochet

Body (single crochet)—Color Group B

1st row	7 stitches	⬥x7
2nd row	14 stitches	⬥x7
3rd row	21 stitches	(⬥x1 + ⬥x1) x7
4th row	28 stitches	(⬥x2 + ⬥x1) x7
5th row	35 stitches	(⬥x3 + ⬥x1) x7
6th row	42 stitches	(⬥x4 + ⬥x1) x7
7th row	49 stitches	(⬥x5 + ⬥x1) x7
8th–17th rows	49 stitches	⬥x49
18th row	42 stitches	(⬥x1 + ⬥x5) x7
19th–23rd rows	42 stitches	⬥x42
24th row	35 stitches	(⬥x1 + ⬥x4) x7
25th–26th rows	35 stitches	⬥x35
27th row	28 stitches	(⬥x1 + ⬥x3) x7
28th row	28 stitches	⬥x28 ●—

Color Table

	Doll 1	Doll 2
Color Group A (head, arms, feet, tail)	Mixed pink + Pink	Mixed light brown + Light brown
Color Group B (main body, ears)	Pale Blue	Light brown
Color Group C (nose, tips of arms and feet)	Plain	Pink

How to Crochet
Arms (single crochet), 2 pieces

			Color Group
1st row	5 stitches	♀ x5	C
2nd row	10 stitches	♧ x10	C
3rd row	15 stitches	(♀ x1 + ♧ x1) x5	C
4th row	20 stitches	(♀ x2 + ♧ x1) x5	C
5th row	10 stitches	♣ x10	A
6th–15th rows	10 stitches	♀ x10 ●—	A

How to Crochet
Legs (single crochet), 2 pieces

			Color Group
1st row	7 stitches	♀ x7	C
2nd row	14 stitches	♧ x7	C
3rd row	21 stitches	(♀ x1 + ♧ x1) x7	C
4th row	28 stitches	(♀ x2 + ♧ x1) x7	C
5th row	14 stitches	♣ x14	A
6th–13th rows	14 stitches	♀ x14 ●—	A

How to Crochet
Ears (single crochet)—Color Group B, 2 pieces

1st row	7 stitches	♀ x7
2nd row	14 stitches	♧ x7
3rd row	21 stitches	(♀ x1 + ♧ x1) x7
4th–14th rows	21 stitches	♀ x21 ●—

How to Crochet
Nose (single crochet)—Color Group C

1st row	6 stitches	♀ x6
2nd row	12 stitches	♧ x6
3rd row	18 stitches	(♀ x1 + ♧ x1) x6
4th row	18 stitches	♀ x18 ●—

How to Crochet
Tail (single crochet)—Color Group A

1st row	6 stitches	♀ x6
2nd row	12 stitches	♧ x6
3rd row	12 stitches	♀ x12
4th row	8 stitches	(♣ x1 + ♀ x1) x4 ●—

Assembling the Body Parts (refer to page 51)

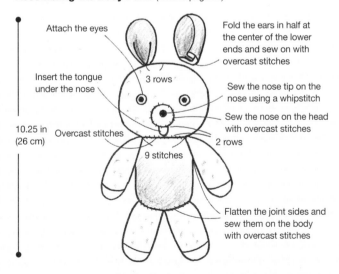

Attach the eyes

Fold the ears in half at the center of the lower ends and sew on with overcast stitches

Insert the tongue under the nose

3 rows

Sew the nose tip on the nose using a whipstitch

Sew the nose on the head with overcast stitches

2 rows

10.25 in (26 cm)

Overcast stitches

9 stitches

Flatten the joint sides and sew them on the body with overcast stitches

Stuff cotton into every body part except for the ears and nose; Do not stuff cotton around the joint parts of the arms and legs

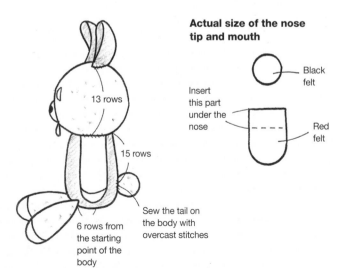

13 rows

15 rows

6 rows from the starting point of the body

Sew the tail on the body with overcast stitches

Actual size of the nose tip and mouth

Black felt

Insert this part under the nose

Red felt

● Citron Puppy

See pages 18–19 for photos.

Yarns

Heavy type
Yellow, 2 oz (55 g)
Blue, 1.4 oz (40 g)
Off-white, 1.4 oz (40 g)
Medium type
Black, 0.4 oz (10 g)

Tools

Size 1 (2.5 mm) and 2 (3 mm)
  crochet hooks
Tapestry needle

Other materials

1 pair of yellow washer beads for 0.4 in
  (1.1 cm) eyes
White felt, 1.6 in × 1.6 in (4 cm × 4 cm)
Small piece of red felt
Synthetic cotton, 2.1 oz (60 g)

Tips

Pick up a single strand of yarn and start from a foundation ring. Work on the ears, nose tip, and tail using a size 1 (2.5 mm) hook and the other parts with a size 2 (3 mm) hook. Stitch every part with a single crochet except for the collar. Sew the collar with post stitches from the last stitch in the head. Leave a long tail at the end and fasten off. Stuff cotton in every body part except for the ears and nose. Use overcast stitches to attach the ears, nose, eyes, head, arms, legs, and tail. Sew the ears and nose onto the head, then attach the eyes. Sew the head, arms, and legs onto the body, then the tail. Sew on the belt.

How to Crochet

Head (single crochet)—Yellow

1st row	7 stitches	×7
2nd row	14 stitches	×7
3rd row	21 stitches	(×1 + ×1) ×7
4th row	28 stitches	(×2 + ×1) ×7
5th row	35 stitches	(×3 + ×1) ×7
6th row	42 stitches	(×4 + ×1) ×7
7th row	49 stitches	(×5 + ×1) ×7
8th row	56 stitches	(×6 + ×1) ×7
9th row	63 stitches	(×7 + ×1) ×7
10th row	70 stitches	(×8 + ×1) ×7
11th row	77 stitches	(×9 + ×1) ×7
12th–16th rows	77 stitches	×77
17th row	70 stitches	(×1 + ×9) ×7
18th row	70 stitches	×70
19th row	63 stitches	(×1 + ×8) ×7
20th row	63 stitches	×63
21st row	56 stitches	(×1 + ×7) ×7
22nd row	56 stitches	×56
23rd row	49 stitches	(×1 + ×6) ×7
24th row	49 stitches	×49
25th row	42 stitches	(×1 + ×5) ×7
26th row	42 stitches	×42
27th row	35 stitches	(×1 + ×4) ×7
28th row	35 stitches	×35
29th row	28 stitches	(×1 + ×3) ×7
30th row	28 stitches	×28
31st row	21 stitches	(×1 + ×2) ×7
32nd row	18 stitches	(×1 + ×5) ×3
33rd–35th rows	18 stitches	×18

How to Crochet

Body (single crochet)

1st row	7 stitches	×7	Blue
2nd row	14 stitches	×7	Blue
3rd row	21 stitches	(×1 + ×1) ×7	Blue
4th row	28 stitches	(×2 + ×1) ×7	Blue
5th row	35 stitches	(×3 + ×1) ×7	Blue
6th row	42 stitches	(×4 + ×1) ×7	Blue
7th row	49 stitches	(×5 + ×1) ×7	Blue
8th row	56 stitches	(×6 + ×1) ×7	Blue
9th–11th rows	56 stitches	×56	Blue
12th row	49 stitches	(×1 + ×6) ×7	Blue
13th row	49 stitches	×49	Blue
14th row	42 stitches	(×1 + ×5) ×7	Blue
15th row	42 stitches	×42	Blue
16th–17th rows	42 stitches	×42	Off-white
18th row	35 stitches	(×1 + ×4) ×7	Off-white
19th–21st rows	35 stitches	×35	Off-white
22nd row	30 stitches	(×1 + ×5) ×5	Off-white
23rd–24th rows	30 stitches	×30	Off-white
25th row	28 stitches	(×1 + ×13) ×2	Off-white
26th–27th rows	28 stitches	×28	Off-white
28th row	24 stitches	(×1 + ×5) ×4	Off-white
29th–30th rows	24 stitches	×24	Off-white
31st row	21 stitches	(×1 + ×6) ×3	Off-white
32nd row	21 stitches	×21	Off-white
33rd row	18 stitches	(×1 + ×5) ×3	Off-white
34th–38th rows	18 stitches	×18	Off-white

> ### How to Do a Post Stitch
>
> Working in single crochet, place the hook from front to back to front, working around the post of the previous row's stitches.

How to Crochet

Legs (single crochet), 2 pieces

1st row	7 stitches	x7	Yellow	
2nd row	14 stitches	x7	Yellow	
3rd row	21 stitches	(x1 + x1) x7	Yellow	
4th row	28 stitches	(x2 + x1) x7	Yellow	
5th–7th rows	28 stitches	x28	Yellow	
8th row	24 stitches	(x1 + x5) x4	Yellow	
9th row	23 stitches	x22 + x1	Yellow	
10th row	17 stitches	x1 + x15 x1	Yellow	Leave 4 stitches
11th row	14 stitches	x1 + x12 x1	Yellow	
12th row	12 stitches	x1 + x10 x1	Yellow	
13th row	10 stitches	x1 + x8 x1	Yellow	
14th row	8 stitches	x1 + x6 x1	Yellow	
15th row	6 stitches	x1 + x4 x1	Yellow	
16th row	4 stitches	x1 + x2 x1	Yellow	
17th row	2 stitches	x1 + x1	Yellow	
18th row	25 stitches	x25	Blue	Pick up the stitches
19th–21st rows	25 stitches	x25	Blue	
22nd row	24 stitches	x1 + x23	Blue	
23rd row	24 stitches	x24	Blue	
24th row	21 stitches	(x1 + x6) x3	Blue	
25th–26th rows	21 stitches	x21	Blue	
27th row	18 stitches	(x1 + x5) x3	Blue	
28th row	18 stitches	x18	Blue	

(Rows 10th–17th are marked "Sole"; rows 18th–28th are marked "Heel")

The 10th–17th rows are the parts for the sole. Crochet in spirals until the 9th row, and in flat pattern from the 10th–17th rows in order to make the heel. Crochet on the 18th row to stitch the heel and instep by picking up the stitches from the 10th–17th rows.

How to Crochet

Arms (single crochet), 2 pieces

1st row	6 stitches	x6	Yellow
2nd row	12 stitches	x6	Yellow
3rd row	18 stitches	(x1 + x1) x6	Yellow
4th row	24 stitches	(x2 + x1) x6	Yellow
5th–7th rows	24 stitches	x24	Yellow
8th row	18 stitches	(x1 + x2) x6	Yellow
9th row	18 stitches	x18	Yellow
10th row	18 stitches	(x1 + x4) x3	Yellow
11th row	15 stitches	x15	Yellow
12th row	14 stitches	x1 + x13	Off-white
13th–14th rows	14 stitches	x14	Off-white
15th row	13 stitches	x1 + x12	Off-white
16th–17th rows	13 stitches	x13	Off-white
18th row	12 stitches	x1 + x11	Off-white
19th–20th rows	12 stitches	x12	Off-white
21st row	11 stitches	x1 + x10	Off-white
12nd–23rd rows	11 stitches	x11	Off-white
24th row	10 stitches	x1 + x9	Off-white
25th–26th rows	10 stitches	x10	Off-white
27th row	9 stitches	x1 + x8	Off-white
22th–29th rows	9 stitches	x9	Off-white

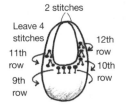

2 stitches

Leave 4 stitches

11th row

9th row

12th row

10th row

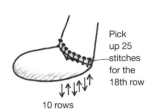

Pick up 25 stitches for the 18th row

10 rows

How to Crochet

Nose tip (single crochet), Black

1st row	7 stitches	x7
2nd–3rd rows	7 stitches	x7

How to Crochet

Tail (single crochet), Black

1st row	5 stitches	x5
2nd row	10 stitches	x5
3rd–8th rows	10 stitches	x10
9th row	9 stitches	x1 + x8
10th–12th rows	9 stitches	x9

How to Crochet

Ears (single crochet), Black

1st row	6 stitches	x6
2nd row	12 stitches	x6
3rd row	18 stitches	(x1 + x1) x6
4th row	21 stitches	(x5 + x1) x3
5th row	21 stitches	x21
6th row	18 stitches	(x1 + x5) x3
7th row	18 stitches	x18
8th row	15 stitches	(x1 + x4) x3
9th–11th rows	15 stitches	x15
12th row	12 stitches	(x1 + x3) x3
13th–14th rows	12 stitches	x12

How to Crochet

Nose (single crochet), Yellow

1st row	7 stitches	x7
2nd row	14 stitches	x7
3rd row	21 stitches	(x1 + x1) x7
4th row	28 stitches	(x2 + x1) x7
5th row	28 stitches	x28
6th row	24 stitches	(x1 + x5) x4
7th row	24 stitches	x24
8th row	21 stitches	(x1 + x6) x3

See page 69 for continuation

● Fluffy Animals

See pages 20–21 for photos.
. . . .

Yarns

Fine mohair type
Doll #1: Navy Blue
Doll #2: White
Doll #3: Gray

Tools

Size 6 (4 mm) crochet hook
Tapestry needle

Other materials

3 pairs of shell buttons for 0.4 in (1 cm)
  eyes
Embroidery threads (see page 20):
  Orange (nose, eye), red (bellybutton,
  eye), yellow green (bellybutton), blue
  (nose, eye, bellybutton), yellow (nose),
  pink (eyes), purple (eye)
Synthetic cotton, 0.4 oz (10 g)

Tips

Pick up a single strand of yarn and start
knitting from a foundation ring with only
single crochet stitches. Leave a long tail
at the end and fasten off. Stuff cotton
into every body part except for the ears
and tail. Use overcast stitches to attach
the ears, nose, eyes, head, arms, legs,
bellybutton, and tail. Sew the ears and
nose onto the head, then attach the eyes.
Sew the head, arms, legs, and bellybutton
onto the body. For doll #2, sew a tail on
its backside.

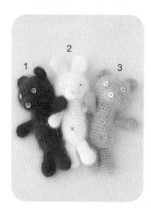

How to Crochet

Head (single crochet)

1st row	7 stitches	❚ x7
2nd row	14 stitches	❤ x7
3rd row	21 stitches	(❚ x1 + ❤ x1) x7
4th row	28 stitches	(❚ x2 + ❤ x1) x7
5th row	35 stitches	(❚ x3 + ❤ x1) x7
6th–10th rows	35 stitches	❚ x35
11th row	28 stitches	(⋏ x1 + ❚ x3) x7
12th row	21 stitches	(⋏ x1 + ❚ x2) x7
13th row	14 stitches	(⋏ x1 + ❚ x1) x7 ●━

How to Crochet

Body (single crochet)

1st row	7 stitches	❚ x7
2nd row	14 stitches	❤ x7
3rd row	21 stitches	(❚ x1 + ❤ x1) x7
4th–9th rows	21 stitches	❚ x21
10th row	18 stitches	(⋏ x1 + ❚ x5) x3
11th row	18 stitches	❚ x18
12th row	15 stitches	(⋏ x1 + ❚ x4) x3
13th row	14 stitches	⋏ x1 + ❚ x13
14th–15th rows	14 stitches	❚ x14 ●━

How to Crochet

Tail (single crochet)
Doll #2

1st row	6 stitches	❚ x6
2nd row	12 stitches	❤ x6
3rd row	12 stitches	❚ x12
4th row	6 stitches	⋏ x6 ●━

How to Crochet

Ears (single crochet), 2 pieces
Dolls #1, #3

1st row	7 stitches	x7
2nd row	14 stitches	x7
3rd row	14 stitches	x14
4th row	9 stitches	(x1 + x1) x4 x1 —

Doll #2

1st row	6 stitches	x6
2nd row	12 stitches	x6
3rd–9th rows	12 stitches	x12 —

How to Crochet

Arms (single crochet), 2 pieces

1st row	6 stitches	x6
2nd row	12 stitches	x6
3rd row	12 stitches	x12
4th row	7 stitches	(x1 + x1 x1) x2 + x1
5th–9th rows	7 stitches	x7 —

How to Crochet

Legs (single crochet), 2 pieces

1st row	7 stitches	x7
2nd row	14 stitches	x7
3rd–5th rows	14 stitches	x14
6th row	9 stitches	(x1 + x1) x4 x1
7th–9th rows	9 stitches	x9 —

How to Crochet

Nose (single crochet)

1st row	6 stitches	x6
2nd row	12 stitches	x6
3rd–4th rows	12 stitches	x12 —

Assembling the Body Parts (refer to page 51)

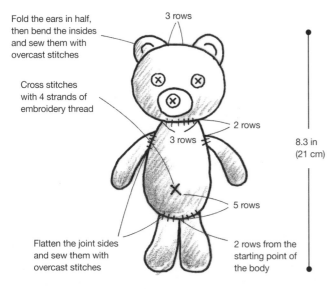

Fold the ears in half, then bend the insides and sew them with overcast stitches

3 rows

Cross stitches with 4 strands of embroidery thread

2 rows

3 rows

Flatten the joint sides and sew them with overcast stitches

5 rows

2 rows from the starting point of the body

8.3 in (21 cm)

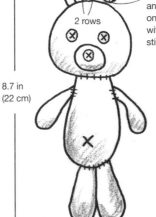

8.7 in (22 cm)

Fold the lower end of the ears in half, and sew them on the head with overcast stitches

2 rows

4 rows from the starting point

How to Attach the Eyes and Nose

Sew a button with 4 strands of embroidery thread, crossing over the thread

Stuff cotton into every body part except for the ears and nose;
Do not stuff cotton around the joint parts of the arms and legs

● Butterflies

See pages 22–23 for photos.

Yarns

Medium type
Doll #1: Orange, 0.7 oz (20 g)
Doll #2: Dark pink, 0.7 oz (20 g)
For both dolls #1 and #2: Yellow, 0.3 oz
  (8 g); Pink, 0.3 oz (8 g); Sky blue, 0.4 oz
  (10 g); Blue green, 0.4 oz (10 g)

Tools

Size 1 (2.2 mm, 2.5 mm) crochet hook
Tapestry needle

Other materials

1 pair each of blue and plain washer
  beads for 0.2 in (0.6 cm) eyes
Red embroidery thread
Synthetic cotton, 0.4 oz (10 g)

Tips

Use a single strand of yarn, and start
with a foundation ring for every body part
except for the wings. To finish the doll,
leave a long tail at the end and fasten off.
Stuff cotton into every body part except
for the wings. Use overcast stitches to
attach the antennae, eyes, mouth, arms,
legs, and wing motifs. Sew the antennae
onto the head. Attach the eyes and
mouth, then the arms and legs. For the
wings, start from a foundation chain and
do single crochets around. Attach the
motifs and sew the wings onto the back.

How to Crochet (refer to Color Table)

Head, Main body and Waist (single crochet)

Row	Stitches		Color Group
1st row	7 stitches	x7	A
2nd row	14 stitches	x7	A
3rd row	21 stitches	(x1 + x1) x7	A
4th row	28 stitches	(x2 + x1) x7	A
5th row	35 stitches	(x3 + x1) x7	A
6th row	35 stitches	x35	A
7th row	35 stitches	x35	A
8th row	35 stitches	x35	B
9th row	35 stitches	x35	B
10th row	35 stitches	x35	B
11th row	28 stitches	(x1 + x3) x7	B
12th row	21 stitches	(x1 + x2) x7	B
13th row	14 stitches	(x1 + x1) x7	B
14th row	12 stitches	(x1 + x5) x2	B
15th–24th rows	12 stitches	x12	B

How to Crochet

Arms (single crochet)—Color Group B, 2 pieces

1st row	5 stitches	x5
2nd row	10 stitches	x5
3rd row	8 stitches	(x1 + x3) x2
4th row	7 stitches	x1 + x6
5th row	6 stitches	x1 + x5
6th–10th rows	6 stitches	x6

How to Crochet

Legs (single crochet)—Color Group B, 2 pieces

1st row	6 stitches	x6
2nd row	12 stitches	x6
3rd row	9 stitches	(x1 + x2) x3
4th row	8 stitches	x1 + x7
5th row	8 stitches	x8
6th row	7 stitches	x1 + x6
7th–10th rows	7 stitches	x7

How to Crochet

Antennae (single crochet)—Color Group A,
2 pieces

1st row	5 stitches	x5
2nd row	10 stitches	x5
3rd row	8 stitches	(x1 + x3) x2
4th row	4 stitches	x4
5th–7th rows	4 stitches	x4

Color Table

	Doll 1	Doll 2
Color Group A (head, waist, wing motifs)	Sky blue	Blue green
Color Group B (main body, wing motifs)	Yellow	Pink
Color Group C (wings)	Orange	Dark pink

How to Crochet

Upper Wings (single crochet)
—Color Group C, 2 pieces

Chains	10 stitches
1st row	26 stitches
2nd row	30 stitches
3rd row	34 stitches
4th row	38 stitches
5th row	38 stitches
6th row	38 stitches
7th row	38 stitches
8th row	34 stitches
9th row	32 stitches
10th row	30 stitches
11th row	28 stitches
12th row	24 stitches
13th row	20 stitches
14th row	16 stitches
15th row	12 stitches

Increase and decrease stitches at both ends of the chains

Upper Wings

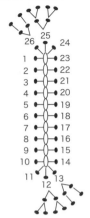

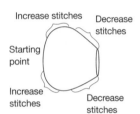

Increase stitches

Decrease stitches

Starting point

Increase stitches

Decrease stitches

How to Crochet

Waist (single crochet)—Color Group B

1st row	6 stitches	x6
2nd row	12 stitches	x6
3rd row	18 stitches (x1 + x1) x6	
4th row	16 stitches (x1 + x7) x2	
5th row	14 stitches (x1 + x6) x2	

How to Crochet

Wing Motifs
Large Circles (single crochet), 4 pieces

1st row	7 stitches	x7
2nd row	14 stitches	x7
3rd row	21 stitches (x1 + x1) x7	

Small Circles (single crochet), 8 pieces

1st row	7 stitches	x7
2nd row	14 stitches	x7

How to Crochet

Lower Wings (single crochet)
—Color Group C, 2 pieces

Chains	5 stitches
1st row	16 stitches
2nd row	20 stitches
3rd row	20 stitches
4th row	20 stitches
5th row	18 stitches
6th row	16 stitches
7th row	16 stitches
8th row	14 stitches
9th row	14 stitches
10th row	12 stitches
11th row	12 stitches
12th row	10 stitches

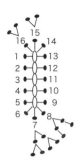

Actual size of the mouth

Chain stitches with 3 strands of red embroidery thread

Assembling the Body Parts (refer to page 51)

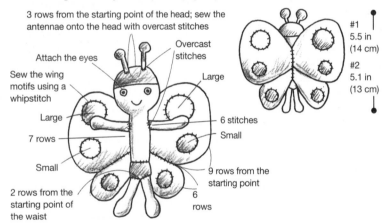

3 rows from the starting point of the head; sew the antennae onto the head with overcast stitches

Overcast stitches

Attach the eyes

Sew the wing motifs using a whipstitch

Large

Large

7 rows

6 stitches

Small

Small

9 rows from the starting point

2 rows from the starting point of the waist

6 rows

#1
5.5 in
(14 cm)

#2
5.1 in
(13 cm)

Stuff cotton into every body part except for the wings;
Do not stuff cotton around the joint parts of the arms and legs

How to Attach the Wings

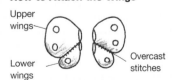

Upper wings

Lower wings

Overcast stitches

Sew the wings onto the back with overcast stitches

Using overcast stitches, sew the hind part that is exposed outside, and attach the rest of the parts onto the back

● Cotton Puppies

See pages 24–25 for photos.

Yarns

Medium cotton type
Doll #1: Light brown, 0.4 oz (10 g); Navy
 blue, 0.4 oz (12 g); White, 0.3 oz (8 g);
 Red, 0.2 oz (5 g)
Doll #2: Pale blue, 0.9 oz (25 g); Light
 Brown 0.2 oz (5 g)

Tools

Size 1 (2.5 mm) crochet hook
Tapestry needle

Other materials

1 pair each of blue and red washer beads
 for 0.2 in (0.6 cm) eyes
Small pieces of black and red felt
Synthetic cotton, 0.4 oz (10 g)
Bell, 1 piece

Tips

Pick up a single strand of yarn and start
from a foundation ring with only single
crochet stitches. To stitch the body, make
a turning chain. Leave a long tail at the
end and fasten off. Stuff cotton into every
body part except for the ears and tail, and
insert a bell inside the head. Use overcast
stitches to attach the ears, nose, eyes,
head, arms, legs, and tail. Sew the ears
and nose onto the head, and attach the
eyes and nose. Sew the head, then the
arms and legs onto the body. Attach the
tail at the back.

How to Crochet (refer to Color Table)

Head (single crochet)—Color Group A

1st row	7 stitches	x7
2nd row	14 stitches	x7
3rd row	21 stitches	(x1 + x1) x7
4th row	28 stitches	(x2 + x1) x7
5th row	35 stitches	(x3 + x1) x7
6th row	42 stitches	(x4 + x1) x7
7th row	49 stitches	(x5 + x1) x7
8th–12th rows	49 stitches	x49
13th row	42 stitches	(x1 + x5) x7
14th row	35 stitches	(x1 + x4) x7
15th row	35 stitches	x35
16th row	28 stitches	(x1 + x3) x7

How to Crochet

Body (single crochet)—Doll #1: Stripes (refer to Color Table);
Doll #2: Color Group A

Row	Stitches		Color Group
1st row	7 stitches	x7	B
2nd row	14 stitches	x7	B
3rd row	21 stitches	(x1 + x1) x7	C
4th row	28 stitches	(x2 + x1) x7	A
5th row	28 stitches	x28	A
6th row	28 stitches	x28	C
7th row	28 stitches	x28	D
8th row	28 stitches	x28	D
9th row	28 stitches	x28	C
10th row	28 stitches	x28	B
11th row	28 stitches	x28	B
12th row	28 stitches	x28	C
13th row	28 stitches	x28	A
14th row	28 stitches	x28	A
15th row	28 stitches	x28	C
16th row	28 stitches	x28	D
17th row	28 stitches	x28	D
18th row	28 stitches	x28	C
19th row	28 stitches	x28	B
20th row	28 stitches	x28	B
21st row	28 stitches	x28	C
22nd row	28 stitches	x28	A

Color Table

	Doll 1	Doll 2
Color Group A (head, main body)	Light brown	Sky blue
Color Group B (nose, tips of arms and feet, striped body)	White	Light brown
Color Group C (Doll #1 ears, arms, legs, striped body)	Navy blue	
Color Group D (Doll #1 striped body)	Red	

How to Crochet

Arms (single crochet), 2 pieces

			Color Group
1st row	6 stitches	↑x6	B
2nd row	12 stitches	⋎x6	B
3rd row	12 stitches	↑x12	B
4th row	10 stitches	(⋏x1 + ↑x4) x2	1-C, 2-A
5th row	10 stitches	↑x10 •—	1-C, 2-A

How to Crochet

Legs (single crochet), 2 pieces

			Color Group
1st row	8 stitches	↑x8	B
2nd row	16 stitches	⋎x8	B
3rd row	16 stitches	↑x16	1-C, 2-A
4th row	14 stitches	(⋏x1 + ↑x6) x2	1-C, 2-A
5th row	14 stitches	↑x14	1-C, 2-A
6th row	14 stitches	↑x14	1-C, 2-A
7th row	12 stitches	(⋏x1 + ↑x5) x2	1-C, 2-A
8th–10th rows	12 stitches	↑x12 •—	1-C, 2-A

How to Crochet

Ears (single crochet)—Doll #1: Color Group C; Doll #2: Color Group A, 2 pieces

1st row	5 stitches	↑x5
2nd row	10 stitches	⋎x5
3rd–7th rows	10 stitches	↑x10 •—

How to Crochet

Nose (single crochet)—Color Group B

1st row	7 stitches	↑x7
2nd row	14 stitches	⋎x7
3rd–4th rows	14 stitches	↑x14 •—

How to Crochet

Tail (single crochet)—Doll #1: Color Group C; Doll #2: Color Group A

1st row	5 stitches	↑x5
2nd–6th rows	5 stitches	↑x5 •—

Assembling the Body Parts (refer to page 51)

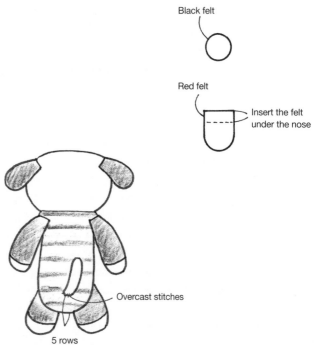

Attach the eyes

6 rows

Flatten the joint sides and sew them on the head with overcast stitches

Insert the tongue under the nose, and attach the pieces with overcast stitches

Overcast stitches

1 row

Sew the nose tip with a whipstitch

5.1 in (13 cm)

Flatten the joint sides and sew them on the body with overcast stitches

6 rows from the starting point of the body

Stuff cotton into every body part except for the ears and tail; Do not stuff cotton around the joint parts of the arms and legs

Overcast stitches

5 rows

Actual size of the nose tip and mouth

Black felt

Red felt

Insert the felt under the nose

● Black and White Kittens

See pages 26–27 for photos.

Yarns

Heavy loop type
Doll #1: Black, 1.4 oz (40 g);
   White, 0.4 oz (10 g)
Doll #2: White, 1.8 oz (50 g)

Tools

Size 2 (3 mm) crochet hook
Tapestry needle

Other materials

1 pair each of washer beads for 0.6 in
   (1.5 cm) eyes: yellow for doll #1, red for
   doll #2
Small pieces of black and red felt
Black embroidery thread
Synthetic cotton, 1.4 oz (40 g)
Bell, 1 piece
Black ribbon for doll #2, W 0.2 in (0.6cm)
   x L 17.7 in (45 cm)

Tips

Pick up a single strand of yarn, and start
from a foundation ring with only single
crochet stitches. Leave a long tail at the
end and fasten off. Stuff cotton into every
body part except for the ears and nose.
Insert the bell in the head. Sew the two
nose parts together, then place the nose
tip in the center using a whipstitch. Use
overcast stitches to attach the tongue,
ears, eyes, arms, legs and tail. Insert the
tongue under the nose and sew it onto
the head. Sew the ears and attach the
eyes. Sew the arms and legs onto the
body, then attach the tail. Use embroidery
thread to sew the whiskers on the nose.
Roll a ribbon around the neck of doll #2,
and tie a bow at the back.

All colors indicated in the tables refer to
Doll #1, except for the white yarns for Doll #2.

How to Crochet

Head (single crochet)—Black

Row	Stitches	Pattern
1st row	7 stitches	x7
2nd row	14 stitches	x7
3rd row	21 stitches	(x1 + x1) x7
4th row	28 stitches	(x2 + x1) x7
5th row	35 stitches	(x3 + x1) x7
6th row	42 stitches	(x4 + x1) x7
7th row	49 stitches	(x5 + x1) x7
8th–11th rows	49 stitches	x49
12th row	42 stitches	(x1 + x5) x7
13th row	35 stitches	(x1 + x4) x7
14th row	35 stitches	x35
15th row	28 stitches	(x1 + x3) x7
16th row	28 stitches	x28
17th row	28 stitches	x28
18th row	21 stitches	(x1 + x2) x7
19th row	18 stitches	(x1 + x5) x3
20th row	18 stitches	x18
21st row	18 stitches	x18

How to Crochet

Body (single crochet)—Black

Row	Stitches	Pattern
1st row	7 stitches	x7
2nd row	14 stitches	x7
3rd row	21 stitches	(x1 + x1) x7
4th row	28 stitches	(x2 + x1) x7
5th row	35 stitches	(x3 + x1) x7
6th–8th rows	35 stitches	x35
9th row	28 stitches	(x1 + x3) x7
10th–15th rows	28 stitches	x28
16th row	21 stitches	(x1 + x2) x7
17th–19th rows	21 stitches	x21
20th row	18 stitches	(x1 + x5) x3
21st–23rd rows	18 stitches	x18
24th row	18 stitches	x18

How to Crochet

Ears (single crochet)—Black, 2 pieces

Row	Stitches	Pattern
1st row	6 stitches	x6
2nd row	6 stitches	x6
3rd row	12 stitches	x6
4th row	12 stitches	x12
5th row	14 stitches	(x5 + x1) x2

How to Crochet

Arms (single crochet), 2 pieces

1st row	5 stitches	⬤ x5		White
2nd row	10 stitches	⬤ x5		White
3rd row	15 stitches	(⬤ x1 + ⬤ x1) x5		White
4th row	15 stitches	⬤ x15		White
5th row	14 stitches	⬤ x1 + ⬤ x13		White
6th row	10 stitches	(⬤ x1 + ⬤ x1) x4 + ⬤ x2		White
7th–14th rows	10 stitches	⬤ x10		Black
15th–20th rows	9 stitches	⬤ x1 + ⬤ x8 ●—		Black

How to Crochet

Nose (single crochet)—White, 2 parts

Row	Stitches	Pattern	
1st–3rd rows	10 stitches	⬤ x10	
4th row	5 stitches	⬤ x5 ●—	

How to Crochet

Legs (single crochet), 2 pieces

1st row	7 stitches	⬤ x7			White
2nd row	14 stitches	⬤ x7			White
3rd row	14 stitches	⬤ x14			White
4th row	14 stitches	⬤ x14			White
5th row	13 stitches	⬤ x12 + ⬤ x1			White
→ 6th row	9 stitches	⬤ x1 + ⬤ x7 + ⬤ x1		Leave 2 stitches	White
← 7th row	7 stitches	⬤ x1 + ⬤ x5 + ⬤ x1			White
→ 8th row	5 stitches	⬤ x1 + ⬤ x3 + ⬤ x1			White
← 9th row	3 stitches	⬤ x1 + ⬤ x1 + ⬤ x1			White
10th row	14 stitches	⬤ x14		Pick up stitches	White
11th row	14 stitches	⬤ x14			White
12th row	13 stitches	⬤ x1 + ⬤ x12			White
13th row	13 stitches	⬤ x13			Black
14th row	12 stitches	⬤ x1 + ⬤ x11			Black
15th–20th rows	12 stitches	⬤ x12 ●—			Black

Crochet in spirals until the 5th row and in flat pattern from the 6th–9th rows in order to make a heel. Work on the 10th row to stitch the heel and instep by picking up stitches from the 5th–9th rows. (Refer to page 59.)

How to Crochet

Tail (single crochet)—Black

Row	Stitches	Pattern	
1st row	8 stitches	⬤ x8	
2nd–14th rows	8 stitches	⬤ x8 ●—	

Assembling the Body Parts (refer to page 51)

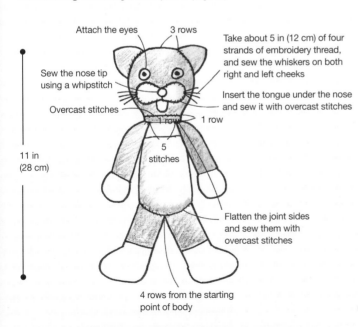

Attach the eyes

3 rows

Take about 5 in (12 cm) of four strands of embroidery thread, and sew the whiskers on both right and left cheeks

Sew the nose tip using a whipstitch

Insert the tongue under the nose and sew it with overcast stitches

Overcast stitches

1 row   1 row

5 stitches

11 in (28 cm)

Flatten the joint sides and sew them with overcast stitches

4 rows from the starting point of body

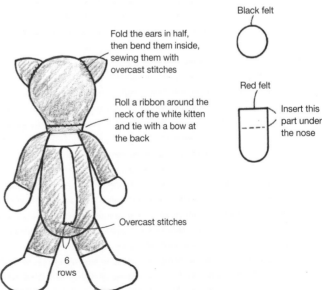

Fold the ears in half, then bend them inside, sewing them with overcast stitches

Roll a ribbon around the neck of the white kitten and tie with a bow at the back

Overcast stitches

6 rows

Actual size of the nose tip and tongue

Black felt

Red felt

Insert this part under the nose

Stuff cotton into every body part except for the ears and nose;
Do not stuff cotton around the joint parts of the arms and legs

● Frogs on Holiday
See pages 28–29 for photos.

Yarns

Heavy loop type
Doll #1: Yellow green, 2.3 oz (65 g);
   Dark green, 0.4 oz (10 g)
Doll #2: Brown, 2.3 oz (65 g);
   Yellow green, 0.4 oz (10 g)
Doll #3: Dark green, 2.3 oz (65 g);
   Yellow green, 0.4 oz (10 g)

Tools

Size 2 (3 mm) crochet hook
Tapestry needle

Other materials

3 pairs of green washer beads for 0.6 in
   (1.5 cm) eyes
Red felt, W 0.8 in (2 cm) × L 2.6 in
   (6.5 cm)
Red embroidery thread
Synthetic cotton, 1.4 oz (40 g)
Bell, 1 piece

Tips

Pick up a single strand of yarn, and start from a foundation ring with only single crochet stitches. Leave a long tail at the end and fasten off. Stuff cotton into every body part and insert the bell in the head. Use overcast stitches to attach the eyes, mouth, arms, and legs. Sew the bases for the eyes onto the head, then attach the eyes and mouth. Sew the arms and legs onto the body.

How to Crochet (refer to Color Table)

Head (single crochet)—Color Group A

1st row	7 stitches	x7
2nd row	14 stitches	x7
3rd row	21 stitches	(x1 + x1) x7
4th row	28 stitches	(x2 + x1) x7
5th row	35 stitches	(x3 + x1) x7
6th row	42 stitches	(x4 + x1) x7
7th row	49 stitches	(x5 + x1) x7
8th row	56 stitches	(x6 + x1) x7
9th row	63 stitches	(x7 + x1) x7
10th row	70 stitches	(x8 + x1) x7
11th–14th rows	70 stitches	x70
15th row	63 stitches	(x1 + x8) x7
16th row	56 stitches	(x1 + x7) x7
17th row	49 stitches	(x1 + x6) x7
18th row	42 stitches	(x1 + x5) x7
19th row	28 stitches	(x1 + x1) x14
20th row	24 stitches	(x1 + x5) x4

How to Crochet

Body (single crochet)—Color Group A

1st row	7 stitches	x7
2nd row	14 stitches	x7
3rd row	21 stitches	(x1 + x1) x7
4th row	28 stitches	(x2 + x1) x7
5th row	35 stitches	(x3 + x1) x7
6th row	42 stitches	(x4 + x1) x7
7th–13th rows	42 stitches	x42
14th row	35 stitches	(x1 + x4) x7
15th–20th rows	35 stitches	x35
21st row	28 stitches	(x1 + x3) x7
22nd–26th rows	28 stitches	x28
27th row	24 stitches	(x1 + x5) x4

How to Crochet

Arms (single crochet), 2 pieces

1st row	6 stitches	x6	B
2nd row	12 stitches	x6	B
3rd row	18 stitches	(x1 + x1) x6	B
4th-6th rows	18 stitches	x18	B
7th row	12 stitches	(x1 + x1) x6	B
8th-30th rows	12 stitches	x12	A

How to Crochet

Legs (single crochet), 2 pieces

1st row	7 stitches	x7	B
2nd row	14 stitches	x7	B
3rd row	21 stitches	(x1 + x1) x7	B
4th–7th rows	21 stitches	x21	B
8th row	14 stitches	(x1 + x1) x7	B
9th–28th rows	14 stitches	x14	A

How to Crochet

Bases for the eyes (single crochet)—Color Group A, 2 pieces

1st row	7 stitches	x7
2nd row	14 stitches	x7
3rd row	21 stitches	(x1 + x1) x7
4th row	21 stitches	x21
5th row	21 stitches	x21

Assembling the Body Parts (refer to page 51)

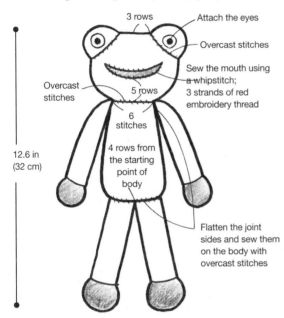

3 rows

Attach the eyes

Overcast stitches

Overcast stitches

5 rows

Sew the mouth using a whipstitch; 3 strands of red embroidery thread

6 stitches

4 rows from the starting point of body

12.6 in (32 cm)

Flatten the joint sides and sew them on the body with overcast stitches

Do not stuff cotton around the joint parts of the arms and legs

Actual size of the mouth

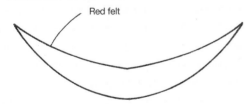

Red felt

● **Continuation of page 59, Citron Puppy**

Belt (single crochet)—Blue

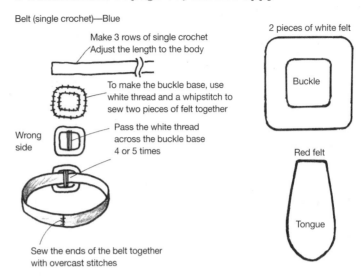

Make 3 rows of single crochet Adjust the length to the body

To make the buckle base, use white thread and a whipstitch to sew two pieces of felt together

Wrong side

Pass the white thread across the buckle base 4 or 5 times

Sew the ends of the belt together with overcast stitches

2 pieces of white felt

Buckle

Red felt

Tongue

How to Crochet

Collar (post stitch + single crochet)—Off-white

1st row	18 stitches	x18
2nd row	24 stitches	(x2 + x1) x6
3rd–4th rows	24 stitches	x24

Stitch the first row by picking up single crochet stitches in the last row of the head (post stitch). Hold the head down so that the front side comes out.

Assembling the Body Parts (refer to page 51)

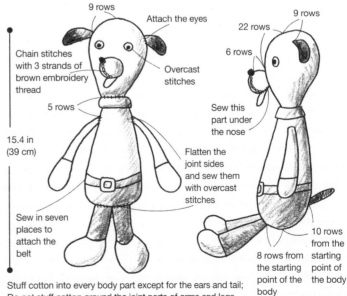

9 rows

Attach the eyes

Chain stitches with 3 strands of brown embroidery thread

Overcast stitches

5 rows

15.4 in (39 cm)

Flatten the joint sides and sew them with overcast stitches

Sew in seven places to attach the belt

9 rows

22 rows

6 rows

Sew this part under the nose

10 rows from the starting point of the body

8 rows from the starting point of the body

Stuff cotton into every body part except for the ears and tail; Do not stuff cotton around the joint parts of arms and legs

● Little Duckling

See pages 30–31 for photos.

Yarns

Medium type

Doll #1: Mustard yellow, 0.9 oz (25 g);
 Orange, 0.2 oz (5 g)

Doll #2: Golden yellow, 0.9 oz (25 g);
 Orange, 0.2 oz (5 g)

Tools

Size 1 (2.5 mm) crochet hook

Tapestry needle

Other materials

2 pairs of orange washer beads for
 0.2 in (0.6 cm) eyes

Synthetic cotton, 0.4 oz (10 g)

Tips

Pick up a single strand of yarn, and start with a single crochet from a foundation ring for all the parts except the bill, which should be stitched from the chains. Leave a long tail at the end and fasten off. Stuff cotton into every body part except for the bill and wings. Insert the eyes, bill, and fringe. Use overcast stitches for the head, wings, and legs. Sew the head onto the body. For doll #1, set the centerlines onto the head and body differently so that the head turns slightly. Sew the wings and legs onto the body.

For Doll #1, use mustard yellow for Color Group A; for Doll #2, use golden yellow for Color Group A

How to Crochet

Head (single crochet)—Color Group A

Row	Stitches	Pattern
1st row	7 stitches	[sc] x7
2nd row	14 stitches	[inc] x7
3rd row	21 stitches	([sc] x1 + [inc] x1) x7
4th row	28 stitches	([sc] x2 + [inc] x1) x7
5th row	35 stitches	([sc] x3 + [inc] x1) x7
6th row	42 stitches	([sc] x4 + [inc] x1) x7
7th row	49 stitches	([sc] x5 + [inc] x1) x7
8th–11th rows	49 stitches	[sc] x49
12th row	42 stitches	([dec] x1 + [sc] x5) x7
13th row	35 stitches	([dec] x1 + [sc] x4) x7
14th row	28 stitches	([dec] x1 + [sc] x3) x7
15th row	21 stitches	([dec] x1 + [sc] x2) x7
16th row	18 stitches	([dec] x1 + [sc] x5) x3 [close]

How to Crochet

Body (single crochet)—Color Group A

Row	Stitches	Pattern
1st row	7 stitches	[sc] x7
2nd row	14 stitches	[inc] x7
3rd row	21 stitches	([sc] x1 + [inc] x1) x7
4th row	28 stitches	([sc] x2 + [inc] x1) x7
5th row	35 stitches	([sc] x3 + [inc] x1) x7
6th row	35 stitches	[sc] x35
7th row	35 stitches	[sc] x35
8th row	28 stitches	([dec] x1 + [sc] x3) x7
9th–11th rows	28 stitches	[sc] x28
12th row	21 stitches	([dec] x1 + [sc] x2) x7
13th row	21 stitches	[sc] x21
14th row	21 stitches	[sc] x21
15th row	18 stitches	([dec] x1 + [sc] x5) x3 [close]

How to Attach the Fringe

4 strands

Cut 16 strands of yarn about 3.15 inches (8 cm) in length.

Insert the hook from the lower side of the loop and pull through the thread.

Then, pick up the rest of the pieces of thread on the upper side and pull them through the loop.

How to Crochet

Wings (single crochet)—Color Group A, 2 pieces

1st row	7 stitches	♟ x7
2nd row	7 stitches	♟ x7
3rd row	14 stitches	♟ x7
4th row	14 stitches	♟ x14
5th row	14 stitches	♟ x14
6th row	16 stitches (♟ x6 + ♟ x1) x2
7th row	18 stitches (♟ x7 + ♟ x1) x2
8th row	12 stitches (♟ x1 + ♟ x1) x6
9th row	12 stitches ♟ x12
10th row	9 stitches (♟ x1 + ♟ x2) x3
11th row	9 stitches ♟ x9 ●—

How to Crochet

Tips of the Feet (single crochet), 2 pieces

			Color Group
1st row	6 stitches	♟ x6	B
2nd row	12 stitches	♟ x6	B
3rd row	18 stitches (♟ x1 + ♟ x1) x6		B
4th row	18 stitches	♟ x18	B
5th row	12 stitches (♟ x1 + ♟ x1) x6		B
6th row	9 stitches (♟ x1 + ♟ x2) x3		B
7th row	9 stitches	♟ x9	A
8th row	9 stitches	♟ x9	B
9th row	8 stitches ♟ x1 + ♟ x7		A
10th row	8 stitches	♟ x8	B
11th row	8 stitches	♟ x8 ●—	A

How to Crochet

Bill (single crochet)—Color B

1st row	16 stitches	♟ x16
2nd row	16 stitches	♟ x16
3rd row	18 stitches (♟ x1 + ♟ x7) x2
4th row	20 stitches (♟ x1 + ♟ x8) x2

For the bill, make 16 chains to form a ring, then make a turning chain to continue with single crochets.

20 stitches

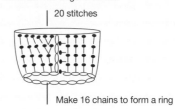

Make 16 chains to form a ring

Assembling the Body Parts (refer to page 51)

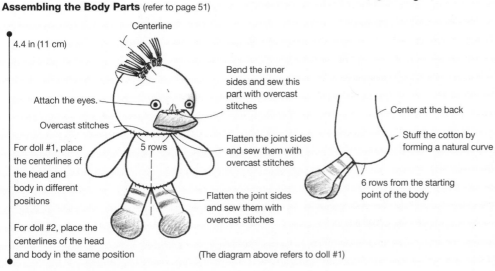

Centerline

4.4 in (11 cm)

Attach the eyes.

Overcast stitches

For doll #1, place the centerlines of the head and body in different positions

For doll #2, place the centerlines of the head and body in the same position

5 rows

Bend the inner sides and sew this part with overcast stitches

Flatten the joint sides and sew them with overcast stitches

Flatten the joint sides and sew them with overcast stitches

(The diagram above refers to doll #1)

Center at the back

Stuff the cotton by forming a natural curve

6 rows from the starting point of the body

Stuff cotton in every part except for the bill and wings; Do not stuff cotton around the joint parts of the legs

● Sheep from Woolen Planet

See pages 32–33 for photos.

Yarns

Medium mohair type, 0.9 oz (25 g)
Doll #1: White
Doll #2: Pale blue

Light baby type, 0.4 oz (10 g)
Both dolls: Sky blue

Tools

Size #1 (2.5 mm) and
 #2 (3 mm) crochet hooks
Tapestry needle

Other materials

2 pairs of blue washer beads for 0.4 in
 (0.9 cm) eyes
Small piece of black felt
Black embroidery thread
Synthetic cotton, 1.1 oz (30 g)
Squeaker, 1 piece

Tips

Pick up a single strand of yarn and use a size #2 (3 mm) crochet hook for the medium yarn and a size #1 (2.5 mm) hook for the light yarn. Start knitting from a foundation ring with only single crochet stitches. Leave a long tail at the end and fasten off. Stuff cotton into every body part except for the ears and tail, and insert a squeaker in the body. Use overcast stitches to attach the ears, nose, forelock, body, eyes, legs, and tail. Sew the ears, nose, and forelock onto the head, then attach the eyes. Sew the lower half of the fore body and hind body, then the upper half onto the head. Attach two legs each onto the fore body and hind body, then sew the tail onto the hind body.

How to Crochet (refer to Color Table)
Head (single crochet)—Color Group A

1st row	7 stitches	x7
2nd row	14 stitches	x7
3rd row	21 stitches	(x1 + x1) x7
4th row	28 stitches	(x2 + x1) x7
5th row	35 stitches	(x3 + x1) x7
6th–13th rows	35 stitches	x35

How to Crochet
Fore body (single crochet)—Color Group A

1st row	7 stitches	x7
2nd row	14 stitches	x7
3rd row	21 stitches	(x1 + x1) x7
4th row	28 stitches	(x2 + x1) x7
5th row	35 stitches	(x3 + x1) x7
6th–8th rows	35 stitches	x35

How to Crochet
Hind body (single crochet)—Color Group A

1st row	7 stitches	x7
2nd row	14 stitches	x7
3rd row	21 stitches	(x1 + x1) x7
4th row	28 stitches	(x2 + x1) x7
5th row	35 stitches	(x3 + x1) x7
6th row	42 stitches	(x4 + x1) x7
7th–9th rows	42 stitches	x42
10th row	35 stitches	(x1 + x4) x7
11th–20th rows	35 stitches	x35

How to Crochet
Tail (single crochet)—Color Group A

1st row	5 stitches	x5
2nd row	7 stitches	(x1 + x1) x2 + x1
3rd row	9 stitches	(x2 + x1) x2 + x1
4th row	9 stitches	x9
5th row	9 stitches	x9

Color Table	Doll 1	Doll 2
Color Group A (head, main body)	White	Pale blue
Color Group B (face, tips of the feet)	Sky blue	Sky blue

How to Crochet

Tips of the Feet (single crochet), 4 pieces

			Color Group
1st row	7 stitches	x7	B
2nd row	14 stitches	x7	B
3rd row	14 stitches	x14	B
4th row	14 stitches	x14	B
5th row	13 stitches	x12 + x1	B
➤ 6th row	9 stitches	x1 + x7 + x1 Leave 2 stitches	B
◄ 7th row	7 stitches	x1 + x5 + x1	B
➤ 8th row	5 stitches	x1 + x3 + x1	B
◄ 9th row	3 stitches	x1 + x1 + x1	B
10th row	14 stitches	x14 Pick up the stitches	B
11th row	14 stitches	x14	B
12th row	13 stitches	x1 + x12	B
13th–15th rows	13 stitches	x13	B
16th–18th rows	13 stitches	x13	A

Crochet in spirals until the 5th row and in flat pattern from the 6th–9th rows in order to make a heel. Work on the 10th row to stitch the heel and instep by picking up the stitches from the 5th–9th rows. (Refer to page 59.)
Turn the insides out to sew from the 16th row and onward for Color Group A.

How to Crochet

Nose (single crochet)—Color Group A, 2 pieces

1st row	7 stitches	x7
2nd row	14 stitches	x7
3rd row	21 stitches	(x1 + x1) x7
4th row	21 stitches	x21

How to Crochet

Ears (single crochet)—Color Group B

1st row	5 stitches	x5
2nd row	10 stitches	x5
3rd row	10 stitches	x10
4th row	10 stitches	x10
5th row	8 stitches	(x1 + x3) x2
6th row	8 stitches	x8
7th row	8 stitches	x8

How to Crochet

Forelock (single crochet)—Color Group A

1st row	6 stitches	x6
2nd row	12 stitches	x6
3rd row	12 stitches	x12

How to Crochet

Face (single crochet)—Color Group B

1st row	7 stitches	x7
2nd row	14 stitches	x7
3rd row	21 stitches	(x1 + x1) x7
4th row	28 stitches	(x2 + x1) x7
5th row	35 stitches	(x3 + x1) x7
6th row	42 stitches	(x4 + x1) x7
7th row	42 stitches	x42

Assembling the Body Parts (refer to page 51)

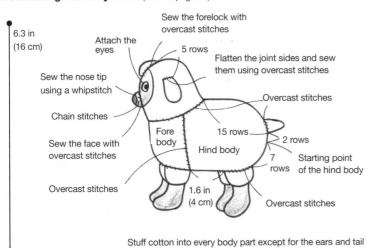

6.3 in (16 cm)

Sew the forelock with overcast stitches

Attach the eyes

5 rows

Flatten the joint sides and sew them using overcast stitches

Sew the nose tip using a whipstitch

Overcast stitches

Chain stitches

Fore body

Hind body

15 rows

2 rows

Sew the face with overcast stitches

7 rows

Starting point of the hind body

Overcast stitches

1.6 in (4 cm)

Overcast stitches

Stuff cotton into every body part except for the ears and tail

Actual size of the nose tip and mouth

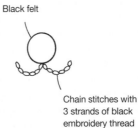

Black felt

Chain stitches with 3 strands of black embroidery thread

● Cotton Candy Elephants

See pages 34–35 for photos.

Yarns

Extra bulky napping type
Doll #1: Pink, 4.6 oz (130 g); Pale blue,
  0.4 oz (10 g); Gray, 0.1 oz (3 g)
Doll #2: Pale blue, 3.2 oz (90 g); Gray,
  1.5 oz (43 g); Sky blue, 0.4 oz (10 g)

Tools

Size #10 (6 mm) crochet hook
Tapestry needle

Other materials

1 pair each of washer beads for 0.6 in
  (1.5 cm) eyes: red for doll #1; blue for
  doll #2
Small piece of red felt
Blue ribbon for doll #2, W 0.2 in (0.5 cm) x
  L 27.6 in (70 cm)
Synthetic cotton, 1.8 oz (50 g)
Bell, 1 piece

Tips

Pick up a single strand of yarn and start
from a foundation ring for all the body parts
except for the tail. Use only single crochet
stitches. Start the tail from the chains.
Leave a long tail at the end and fasten off.
Stuff cotton into every body part except for
the ears, and insert a bell inside the head.
Use overcast stitches to attach the ears,
nose, eyes, tongue, head, arms, and legs.
Sew the ears and nose onto the head and
attach the eyes and tongue. Sew the head
onto the body, then the arms and legs. Sew
the tail at the back of the body. For doll #2,
roll the ribbon around the neck and tie a
bow at the back.

How to Crochet (refer to Color Table)
Head (single crochet)—Color Group A

Row	Stitches	Pattern
1st row	8 stitches	x8
2nd row	16 stitches	x8
3rd row	24 stitches	(x1 + x1) x8
4th row	32 stitches	(x2 + x1) x8
5th row	40 stitches	(x3 + x1) x8
6th–10th rows	40 stitches	x40
11th row	32 stitches	(x1 + x3) x8
12th row	24 stitches	(x1 + x2) x8
13th row	21 stitches	(x1 + x6) x3 ●

How to Crochet
Body (single crochet)—Color Group A

Row	Stitches	Pattern
1st row	8 stitches	x8
2nd row	16 stitches	x8
3rd row	24 stitches	(x1 + x1) x8
4th–11th rows	24 stitches	x24
12th row	21 stitches	(x1 + x6) x3
13th row	21 stitches	x21
14th row	21 stitches	x21 ●

Color Table		Doll 1	Doll 2
Color Group A (head, main body, arms, legs, tail)		Pink	Pale blue
Color Group B (tips of the arms and feet, tail)		Pale blue	Sky blue
Color Group C (tips of the nose, arms, legs)		Gray	Gray

How to Crochet

Arms (single crochet)—2 pieces

			Color Group
1st row	7 stitches	x7	B
2nd row	14 stitches	x7	B
3rd–7th rows	14 stitches	x14	1-A, 2-C
8th row	13 stitches	x1 + x12	1-A, 2-C
9th row	13 stitches	x13	1-A, 2-C

How to Crochet

Legs (single crochet)—2 pieces

			Color Group
1st row	8 stitches	x8	B
2nd row	16 stitches	x8	B
3rd–7th rows	16 stitches	x16	1-A, 2-C
8th row	15 stitches	x1 + x14	1-A, 2-C
9th row	15 stitches	x15	1-A, 2-C

How to Crochet

Ears (single crochet)—Color Group A, 2 pieces

1st row	8 stitches	x8
2nd row	16 stitches	x8
3rd row	24 stitches	(x1+ x1) x8

How to Crochet

Nose (single crochet)

			Color Group
1st row	6 stitches	x6	C
2nd row	12 stitches	x6	C
3rd row	10 stitches	(x1 + x4) x2	A
4th–9th rows	10 stitches	x10	A

How to Crochet

Tail (single crochet)—Doll #1: Color Group A; Doll #2: Color Group B

Make 4 chains and a turning chain to continue
4 single crochet stitches.

Assembling the Body Parts (refer to page 51)

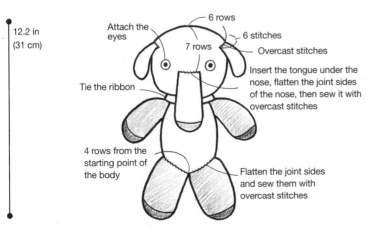

12.2 in
(31 cm)

Attach the eyes

6 rows

6 stitches

7 rows

Overcast stitches

Insert the tongue under the nose, flatten the joint sides of the nose, then sew it with overcast stitches

Tie the ribbon

4 rows from the starting point of the body

Flatten the joint sides and sew them with overcast stitches

Stuff cotton into every body part except for the ears;
Do not stuff cotton around the joint parts of the arms and legs

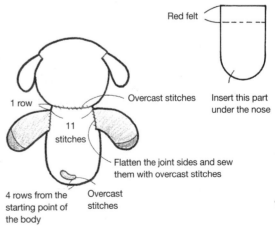

1 row

11 stitches

Overcast stitches

4 rows from the starting point of the body

Overcast stitches

Flatten the joint sides and sew them with overcast stitches

Actual size of the tongue

Red felt

Insert this part under the nose

● American Lions

See pages 36–37 for photos.

· ·

Yarns

Extra bulky type
Doll #1: Light brown, 2.8 oz (80 g);
  Golden yellow, 1.4 oz (40 g); Red,
  0.5 oz (15 g)
Doll #2: Golden yellow, 2.8 oz (80 g);
  Light brown, 1.4 oz (40 g); Sky blue
  0.5 oz (15 g)

Medium type
For both dolls: Black thread

Tools

Size #6 (4 mm) crochet hook
Tapestry needle

Other materials

1 pair each of orange washer beads for
  0.5 in (1.2 cm) eyes
Black embroidery thread
Synthetic cotton, 2.8 oz (80 g)
Bell, 1 piece
Squeaker, 1 piece

Tips

Pick up a single strand of yarn and start
from a foundation ring with only single
crochet stitches. Leave a long tail at the
end and fasten off. Stuff cotton into every
body part except for the ears, nose, and
tail. Insert a bell inside the head and a
squeaker in the body. Use overcast stitches
to attach the ears, nose, eyes, arms, legs,
and tail. Sew the ears and nose onto the
head, then attach the eyes. Sew the arms
and legs onto body, then attach the tail at
the back. To make the mane, first work on
one row with a single crochet around the
face, then place the fringe over it. (Refer to
page 70 for instructions on making fringe.)
When the mane is completed all around the
head, trim the tips to arrange them. Attach
the whiskers. Attach a pom pom at the tip
of the tail.

1   2

How to Crochet (refer to Color Table)

Head (single crochet)—Color Group A

1st row	7 stitches	x7
2nd row	14 stitches	x7
3rd row	21 stitches	(x1 + x1) x7
4th row	28 stitches	(x2 + x1) x7
5th row	35 stitches	(x3 + x1) x7
6th row	42 stitches	(x4 + x1) x7
7th–10th rows	42 stitches	x42
11th row	35 stitches	(x1 + x4) x7
12th row	28 stitches	(x1 + x3) x7
13th row	21 stitches	(x1 + x2) x7
14th row	18 stitches	(x1 + x5) x3
15th row	18 stitches	x18
16th row	18 stitches	x18

How to Crochet

Body (single crochet)—Color Group A

1st row	7 stitches	x7
2nd row	14 stitches	x7
3rd row	21 stitches	(x1 + x1) x7
4th row	28 stitches	(x2 + x1) x7
5th–7th rows	28 stitches	(x28
8th row	28 stitches	(x1 + x2) x7
9th–13th rows	21 stitches	x21
14th row	21 stitches	(x1 + x5) x3
15th–17th rows	18 stitches	x18

How to Crochet

Arms (Single crochet), 2 pieces

			Color Group
1st row	6 stitches	x6	B
2nd row	12 stitches	x6	B
3rd row	12 stitches	x12	B
4th row	8 stitches	(x1 + x1) x4	B
5th row	8 stitches	x8	B
6th–8th rows	8 stitches	x8	A
8th row	7 stitches	x1+ x6	A
10th–16th rows	7 stitches	x7	A

Color Table

Color Group A (head, main body, arms, legs, tail)
Color Group B (tips of the arms and feet, nose)
Color Group C (mane, tail's pom pom)

	Doll 1	Doll 2
Color Group A	Light brown	Golden yellow
Color Group B	Golden yellow	Light brown
Color Group C	Red	Sky blue

How to Crochet

Legs (single crochet), 2 pieces

Row	Stitches	Pattern	Color Group
1st row	7 stitches	×7	B
2nd row	14 stitches	×7	B
3rd–5th rows	14 stitches	×14	B
6th row	13 stitches	×12 + ×1	B
→ 7th row	9 stitches	×1 + ×7 + ×1 Leave 2 stitches	B
← 8th row	7 stitches	×1 + ×5 + ×1	B
→ 9th row	5 stitches	×1 + ×3 + ×1	B
← 10th row	3 stitches	×1 + ×1 + ×1	B
11th row	14 stitches	×14 Pick up the stitches	A
12th row	14 stitches	×14	A
13th row	13 stitches	×1 + ×12	A
14th–16th rows	13 stitches	×13	A
17th row	12 stitches	×1 + ×11 ●	A

Crochet in spirals until the 6th row with yarns of Color Group B, and in flat pattern for the 7th–10th rows in order to make a heel. From the 11th row, use yarns of Color Group A and stitch the heel and instep by picking up the stitches from the 6th–10th rows. (Refer to page 59.)

How to Crochet

Ears (single crochet)—Color Group A, 2 pieces

Row	Stitches	Pattern
1st row	6 stitches	×6
2nd row	12 stitches	×6
3rd row	18 stitches	(×1 + ×1) ×6
4th row	9 stitches	×9 ●

How to Crochet

Tail (single crochet)—Color Group A

Row	Stitches	Pattern
1st row	6 stitches	×6
2nd–9th rows	6 stitches	×6 ●

How to Crochet

Nose (single crochet)—Color Group B, 2 pieces

Row	Stitches	Pattern
1st row	10 stitches	×10
2nd row	10 stitches	×10 ●

How to Crochet

Nose tip (single crochet)—Black

Row	Stitches	Pattern
1st Row	8 stitches	×8 ●

Assembling the Body Parts (refer to page 51)

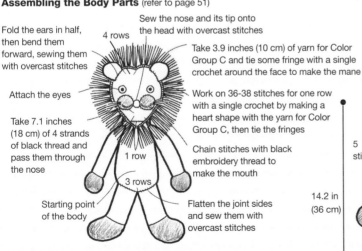

Fold the ears in half, then bend them forward, sewing them with overcast stitches

4 rows

Sew the nose and its tip onto the head with overcast stitches

Take 3.9 inches (10 cm) of yarn for Color Group C and tie some fringe with a single crochet around the face to make the mane

Attach the eyes

Work on 36-38 stitches for one row with a single crochet by making a heart shape with the yarn for Color Group C, then tie the fringes

Take 7.1 inches (18 cm) of 4 strands of black thread and pass them through the nose

Chain stitches with black embroidery thread to make the mouth

1 row

3 rows

Starting point of the body

Flatten the joint sides and sew them with overcast stitches

Stuff cotton into every body part except for the ears, nose, and tail; Do not stuff cotton around the joint parts of the arms and legs

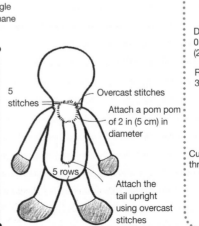

5 stitches

Overcast stitches

Attach a pom pom of 2 in (5 cm) in diameter

14.2 in (36 cm)

5 rows

Attach the tail upright using overcast stitches

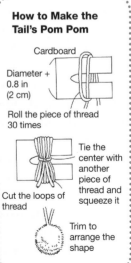

How to Make the Tail's Pom Pom

Cardboard

Diameter + 0.8 in (2 cm)

Roll the piece of thread 30 times

Tie the center with another piece of thread and squeeze it

Cut the loops of thread

Trim to arrange the shape

● Piggies in Love

See pages 38-39 for photos.
· ·

Yarns

Medium mohair type
Doll #1: Pink, 1.1 oz (30 g); Pale reddish
  brown, 0.2 oz (5 g)
Doll #2: Pale reddish brown, 1.1 oz (30 g);
  Pink, 0.2 oz (5 g)

Tools

Size #2 (3 mm) crochet hook
Tapestry needle

Other materials

1 pair each of pink washer beads for
  0.4 in (0.9 cm) eyes
Synthetic cotton, 0.7 oz (20 g)
Squeaker, 1 piece

Tips

Pick up a single strand of yarn and start
from a foundation ring with only single
crochet stitches. Leave a long tail at the
end and fasten off. Stuff cotton into every
body part except for the ears and tail,
then insert a squeaker in the body. Using
overcast stitches, sew the ears and nose
onto the head; attach the eyes; sew the
head, arms, and legs onto the body; and
sew the tail at the back.

1

2

How to Crochet (refer to Color Table)
Head (single crochet)—Color Group A

1st row	7 stitches	♀x7
2nd row	14 stitches	♀x7
3rd row	21 stitches	(♀x1 + ♀x1) x7
4th row	28 stitches	(♀x2 + ♀x1) x7
5th row	35 stitches	(♀x3 + ♀x1) x7
6th row	42 stitches	(♀x4 + ♀x1) x7
7th row	49 stitches	(♀x5 + ♀x1) x7
8th row	56 stitches	(♀x6 + ♀x1) x7
9th–12th rows	56 stitches	♀x56
13th row	49 stitches	(⅄x1 + ♀x6) x7
14th–15th rows	49 stitches	♀x49
16th row	42 stitches	(⅄x1 + ♀x5) x7
17th row	42 stitches	♀x42
18th row	35 stitches	(⅄x1 + ♀x4) x7
19th row	28 stitches	(⅄x1 + ♀x3) x7
20th row	28 stitches	♀x28 ●–

How to Crochet
Body (single crochet)—Color Group A

1st row	7 stitches	♀x7
2nd row	14 stitches	♀x7
3rd row	21 stitches	(♀x1 + ♀x1) x7
4th row	28 stitches	(♀x2 + ♀x1) x7
5th row	28 stitches	♀x28
6th row	28 stitches	♀x28
7th row	35 stitches	(♀x3 + ♀x1) x7
8th row	35 stitches	♀x35
9th row	35 stitches	♀x35
10th row	42 stitches	(♀x4 + ♀x1) x7
11th–13th rows	42 stitches	♀x42
14th row	35 stitches	(⅄x1 + ♀x4) x7
15th–17th rows	35 stitches	♀x35
18th row	28 stitches	(⅄x1 + ♀x3) x7
19th–23th rows	28 stitches	♀x28 ●–

Color Table		Doll 1	Doll 2
Color Group A (head, main body, arms, legs, tail)		Pink	Pale reddish brown
Color Group B (tips of arms and feet, nose)		Pale reddish brown	Pink

How to Crochet

Arms (single crochet), 2 pieces

			Color Group
1st row	5 stitches	⬤x5	B
2nd row	10 stitches	⬤x5	B
3rd row	10 stitches	⬤x10	B
4th–14th rows	10 stitches	⬤x10	A

How to Crochet

Ears (single crochet)—Color Group A, 2 pieces

1st row	5 stitches	⬤x5
2nd row	5 stitches	⬤x5
3rd row	10 stitches	⬤x5
4th row	10 stitches	⬤x10
5th row	15 stitches	(⬤x1 + ⬤x1) x5
6th row	15 stitches	⬤x15 ⬤

How to Crochet

Legs (single crochet)—2 pieces

			Color Group
1st row	7 stitches	⬤x7	B
2nd row	14 stitches	⬤x7	B
3rd row	14 stitches	⬤x14	B
4th–12th rows	14 stitches	⬤x14 ⬤	A

How to Crochet

Nose (single crochet)

			Color Group
1st row	6 stitches	⬤x6	B
2nd row	12 stitches	⬤x6	B
3rd row	12 stitches	⬤x12	B
4th–6th rows	12 stitches	⬤x12 ⬤	A

How to Crochet

Tail (single crochet)—Color Group A

Make 6 chains and a turning chain to continue 6 single crochet stitches.

Assembling the Body Parts (refer to page 51)

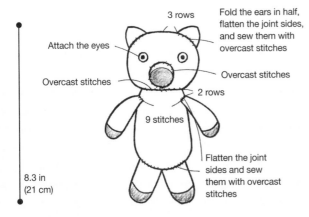

3 rows

Attach the eyes

Fold the ears in half, flatten the joint sides, and sew them with overcast stitches

Overcast stitches

Overcast stitches

2 rows

9 stitches

Flatten the joint sides and sew them with overcast stitches

8.3 in (21 cm)

Attach the tail using overcast stitches

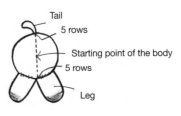

Tail

5 rows

Starting point of the body

5 rows

Leg

Stuff cotton into every body part except for the ears and tail;
Do not stuff cotton around the joint parts of the arms and legs

● Cat-like Tiger

See pages 40–41 for photos.

Yarns

Medium fur type
Doll #1: Yellow, 1.2 oz (35 g); Gray 0.3 oz (8 g)
Doll #2: Orange 1.2 oz (35 g); Gray 0.3 oz (8 g)

Tools

Size #2 (3 mm) crochet hook
Tapestry needle

Other materials

1 pair of yellow washer beads for 0.4 in (1 cm) eyes
Small pieces of red and black felt
Bell, 1 piece
Squeaker, 1 piece
Synthetic cotton, 1.8 oz (50 g)

Tips

Pick up a single strand of yarn and start from a foundation ring with only single crochet stitches. Crochet from a turning chain for the striped parts, paying attention to the alignment of rows when the colors change. Leave a longer tail at the end and fasten off. Stuff cotton into every body part except for the ears and nose, and insert a bell inside the head and a squeaker into the body. To make the nose, sew two parts together and attach the nose tip as you insert the tongue underneath it. Then, sew this part onto the head with overcast stitches. Use overcast stitches to attach the ears, eyes, head, arms, legs, and tail. Sew the ears onto the head and attach the eyes. Sew the head, arms, and legs onto the body, then the tail at the back. Pass the embroidery thread through the nose to make whiskers.

1
2

How to Crochet (refer to Color Table)

Head (single crochet)

			Color Group
1st row	7 stitches	♀ x7	A
2nd row	14 stitches	♀ x7	A
3rd row	21 stitches	(♀ x1 + ♀ x1) x7	B
4th row	28 stitches	(♀ x2 + ♀ x1) x7	A
5th row	35 stitches	(♀ x3 + ♀ x1) x7	A
6th row	42 stitches	(♀ x4 + ♀ x1) x7	B
7th row	49 stitches	(♀ x5 + ♀ x1) x7	A
8th row	49 stitches	♀ x49	A
9th row	49 stitches	♀ x49	B
10th row	49 stitches	♀ x49	A
11th row	49 stitches	♀ x49	A
12th row	49 stitches	♀ x49	B
13th row	42 stitches	(♣ x1 + ♀ x5) x7	A
14th row	35 stitches	(♣ x1 + ♀ x4) x7	A
15th row	28 stitches	(♣ x1 + ♀ x3) x7	B
16th row	21 stitches	(♣ x1 + ♀ x2) x7	A
17th row	21 stitches	♀ x21 ●━	A

How to Crochet

Body (single crochet stripes)

			Color Group
1st row	7 stitches	♀ x7	A
2nd row	14 stitches	♀ x7	A
3rd row	21 stitches	(♀ x1 + ♀ x1) x7	B
4th row	28 stitches	(♀ x2 + ♀ x1) x7	A
5th row	35 stitches	(♀ x3 + ♀ x1) x7	A
6th row	35 stitches	♀ x35	B
7th row	35 stitches	♀ x35	A
8th row	35 stitches	♀ x35	A
9th row	35 stitches	♀ x35	B
10th row	28 stitches	(♣ x1 + ♀ x3) x7	A
11th row	28 stitches	♀ x28	A
12th row	28 stitches	♀ x28	B
13th row	28 stitches	♀ x28	A
14th row	28 stitches	♀ x28	A
15th row	28 stitches	♀ x28	B
16th row	21 stitches	(♣ x1 + ♀ x2) x7	A
17th row	21 stitches	♀ x21	A
18th row	21 stitches	♀ x21	B
19th row	21 stitches	♀ x21	A
20th row	21 stitches	♀ x21	A
21th row	21 stitches	♀ x21	B
22th row	21 stitches	♀ x21 ●━	A

Color Table

	Doll 1	Doll 2
Color Group A (head, main body, arms, legs, tail)	Yellow	Orange
Color Group B (stripes, whiskers)	Gray	Gray

How to Crochet

Arms (single crochet stripes), 2 pieces   Color Group

Row	Stitches	Pattern	Color Group
1st row	6 stitches	×6	A
2nd row	12 stitches	×6	A
3rd row	18 stitches	(×1 + ×1) ×6	A
4th row	18 stitches	×18	A
5th row	12 stitches	(×1 + ×1) ×6	A
6th row	12 stitches	×12	A
7th row	10 stitches	(×1 + ×4) ×2	A
8th–11th rows	10 stitches	×10 (B for 8th and 11th rows)	A
12th row	9 stitches	×1 + ×8	A
13th row	9 stitches	×9	A
14th row	9 stitches	×9	B
15th row	8 stitches	×1 + ×7	A
16th–19th rows	8 stitches	×8 (B for 17th row)	

Crochet in spirals until the 7th row, then make a turning chain to continue from the 8th row and onward.

How to Crochet

Legs (single crochet stripes), 2 pieces   Color Group

Row	Stitches	Pattern	Color Group
1st row	7 stitches	×7	A
2nd row	14 stitches	×7	A
3rd row	21 stitches	(×1 + ×1) ×7	A
4th–6th rows	21 stitches	×21	A
7th row	13 stitches	(×1 + ×1) ×6 + ×1	A
→ 8th row	9 stitches	×1 + ×7 + ×1 Leave 2 stitches	A
← 9th row	7 stitches	×1 + ×5 + ×1	A
→ 10th row	5 stitches	×1 + ×3 + ×1	A
← 11th row	3 stitches	×1 + ×1 + ×1	A
12th row	14 stitches	×14 Pick up the 14 stitches	A
13th–20th rows	14 stitches	×14	*

*Use the yarn of Color Group B for the 13th, 16th, and 19th rows and Color Group A for the rest of the rows.
Crochet in spirals until the 8th row and in flat pattern from the 9th–11th rows in order to make a heel. Work on the 12th row to stitch the heel and instep by picking up the stitches from the 7th–11th rows. (Refer to page 59.) Make a turning chain to continue from the 12th row and onward.

How to Crochet

Ears (single crochet stripes)—Color Group A, 2 parts

Row	Stitches	Pattern
1st row	6 stitches	×6
2nd row	6 stitches	×6
3rd row	12 stitches	×6
4th row	14 stitches	(×5 + ×1) ×2
5th row	14 stitches	×14

How to Crochet

Mouth (single crochet)—Color Group A, 2 parts

Row	Stitches	Pattern
1st row	6 stitches	×6
2nd row	6 stitches	×6
3rd row	12 stitches	×6
4th row	6 stitches	×6
5th row	6 stitches	×6

How to Crochet

Tail (single crochet stripes)

Row	Stitches	Pattern
1st row	8 stitches	×8
2nd–18th rows	8 stitches	×8

*Use the yarn of Color Group B for the 4th, 7th, 10th, 13th, and 16th rows and Color Group A for the rest of the rows.
Make a turning chain to start the tail.

Assembling the Body Parts (refer to page 51)

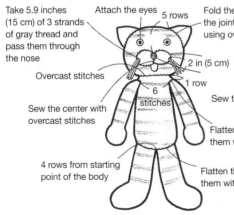

Take 5.9 inches (15 cm) of 3 strands of gray thread and pass them through the nose

Attach the eyes

5 rows

Fold the ears in half, flatten the joint sides and sew them using overcast stitches

Insert the tongue under the nose, and sew it with overcast stitches

Overcast stitches

2 in (5 cm)

1 row

6 stitches

Sew the nose tip with a whipstitch

Sew the center with overcast stitches

Flatten the joint sides and sew them with overcast stitches

4 rows from starting point of the body

Flatten the joint sides and sew them with overcast stitches

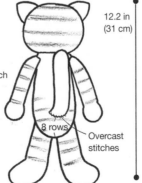

12.2 in (31 cm)

8 rows

Overcast stitches

Actual size of the nose tip and tongue

Black felt   Red felt

Insert this part under the nose

Stuff cotton into every body part except for the ears and nose;
Do not stuff cotton around the joint parts of the arms and legs

● Colorful Donkeys

See pages 42–43 for photos.

Yarns

Bulky type

Doll #1: Brown and dark brown mix,
0.7 oz (20 g); Reddish brown, 0.4 oz
(10 g); Brown and gray mix, 0.4 oz (10 g);
Brown, 0.2 oz (5 g); Gray, 0.2 oz (5 g);
Pale blue, 0.5 oz (15 g); Red, 0.4 oz (15 g)

Doll #2: Gray, 0.9 oz (25 g); Brown and
gray mix, 0.4 oz (10 g); Reddish brown,
0.5 oz (15 g); Pale blue, 0.5 oz (15 g);
Dark pink, 0.4 oz (10 g)

Tools

Size #2 (3 mm) crochet hook
Tapestry needle

Other materials

1 pair each of washer beads for 0.4 in
(0.9 cm) eyes: sky blue and green for
doll #1; red for doll #2
Small piece of black felt
Red embroidery thread
Synthetic cotton, 3.2 oz (90 g)
1 piece each of gingham checkered
fabric, 9.1 in x 9.1 in (23 cm x 23 cm):
green for doll #1; sky blue for doll #2
Bell, 1 piece
Squeaker, 1 piece

Tips

Pick up a single strand of yarn and start
from a foundation ring with only single
crochet stitches. Leave a long tail at the
end and fasten off. Stuff cotton into every
body part except for the ears, then insert
a bell inside the head and a squeaker in
the body. Use overcast stitches to attach
the ears, nose, body, buttocks, head,
legs, and tail. Sew the ears and nose onto
the head, then attach the eyes. Sew the
body and buttocks together, then sew the
head, legs, and tail onto the body. Attach
a pom pom at the tip of the tail, and wrap
a bandana around the neck.

How to Crochet (refer to Color Table)

Head (single crochet)—Color Group A

1st row	7 stitches	x7
2nd row	14 stitches	x7
3rd row	21 stitches	(x1 + x1) x7
4th row	28 stitches	(x2 + x1) x7
5th row	35 stitches	(x3 + x1) x7
6th–9th rows	35 stitches	x35
10th row	28 stitches	(x1 + x3) x7
11th row	28 stitches	x28
12th row	21 stitches	(x1 + x2) x7
13th–24th rows	21 stitches	x21

How to Crochet

Body (single crochet)—Color Group B

1st row	7 stitches	x7
2nd row	14 stitches	x7
3rd row	21 stitches	(x1 + x1) x7
4th row	28 stitches	(x2 + x1) x7
5th–17th rows	28 stitches	x28

Buttocks (single crochet)—Color Group C

1st row	7 stitches	x7
2nd row	14 stitches	x7
3rd row	21 stitches	(x1 + x1) x7
4th row	28 stitches	(x2 + x1) x7
5th–9th rows	28 stitches	x28

Actual size of the nose tip and mouth

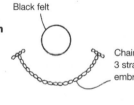

Black felt

Chain stitches with
3 strands of red
embroidery thread

Color Table

	Doll 1	Doll 2
Color Group A (head)	Reddish brown and dark brown mix	Gray
Color Group B (main body)	Reddish brown	Brown and gray mix
Color Group C (buttocks)	Brown	Gray
Color Group D (legs)	Brown and gray mix	Reddish brown
Color Group E (tail)	Gray	Reddish brown
Color Group F (ears)	Red	Dark pink
Color Group G (nose, tips of feet)	Pale blue	Pale blue

How to Crochet

Legs (single crochet), 4 pieces

			Color Group
1st row	6 stitches	●x6	F
2nd row	12 stitches	❤x6	F
3rd row	18 stitches	(●x1 + ❤x1) x6	F
4th row	18 stitches	●x18	G
5th row	18 stitches	● x18	G
6th row	15 stitches	(♣x1 + ●x4) x3	G
7th row	15 stitches	● x15	G
8th–10th rows	15 stitches	●x15	D
11th row	14 stitches	♣x1 + ●x13	D
12th–14th rows	14 stitches	●x14	D
15th row	13 stitches	♣x1 + ●x12	D
16th–18th rows	13 stitches	●x13	D
19th row	12 stitches	♣x1 + ●x11 ●—	D

How to Crochet

Ears (single crochet)—Color Group F, 2 pieces

1st row	6 stitches	●x6
2nd row	6 stitches	●x6
3rd row	12 stitches	❤x6
4th row	14 stitches	(❤x1 + ●x6) x2
5th–6th rows	14 stitches	●x14
7th row	7 stitches	♣x7 ●—

Nose (single crochet)—Color Group G

1st row	7 stitches	●x7
2nd row	14 stitches	❤x7
3rd row	21 stitches	(●x1 + ❤x1) x7
4th row	21 stitches	●x21
5th row	14 stitches	(♣x1 + ●x1) x7
6th row	14 stitches	●x14
7th row	14 stitches	●x14 ●—

Tail (single crochet)—Color Group E

1st row	8 stitches	●x8
2nd row	8 stitches	●x8
3rd row	7 stitches	♣x1 + ●x6
4th row	7 stitches	●x7
5th row	7 stitches	●x7 ●—

Assembling the Body Parts (refer to page 51)

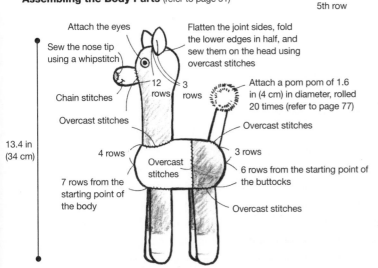

Attach the eyes

Sew the nose tip using a whipstitch

Flatten the joint sides, fold the lower edges in half, and sew them on the head using overcast stitches

Chain stitches

12 rows   3 rows

Attach a pom pom of 1.6 in (4 cm) in diameter, rolled 20 times (refer to page 77)

Overcast stitches

Overcast stitches

13.4 in (34 cm)

4 rows

Overcast stitches

3 rows

6 rows from the starting point of the buttocks

7 rows from the starting point of the body

Overcast stitches

Stuff cotton into every body part except for the ears;
Do not stuff cotton around the joint parts of the legs

How to Fold the Bandanas

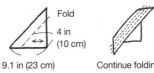

Fold

4 in (10 cm)

9.1 in (23 cm)

Continue folding on the dotted lines

Roll the bandana around the neck

● Boy and Girl

See pages 44–45 for photos.

Yarns

Extra bulky napping type
Doll #1: Moss green, 2.5 oz (70 g);
 Light brown, 1.8 oz (50 g); Navy blue,
 1.1 oz (30 g); Red, 0.7 oz (20 g);
 Plain, 0.7 oz (20 g)

Doll #2: Navy blue, 1.1 oz (30 g);
 Sky blue, 1.1 oz (30 g); Yellow green,
 1.1 oz (30 g); Light brown, 0.7 oz (20 g);
 Plain, 0.7 oz (20 g); Yellow, 0.4 oz (10 g)

Tools

Size #10 (6 mm) crochet hook
Tapestry needle

Other materials

1 pair each of washer beads for 0.6 in
 (1.5 cm) eyes: green for doll #1; blue for
 doll #2
Red embroidery thread
Synthetic cotton, 5.3 oz (150 g)
Bell, 1 piece
Squeaker, 1 piece
Ornament, 1 piece

Tips

Pick up a single strand of yarn and start
from a foundation ring with only single
crochet stitches. To sew the girl, pick
up the stitches of the body to crochet
the skirt. Leave a long tail at the end
and fasten off. Stuff cotton in the body,
and insert a bell inside the head and
a squeaker in the body. Use overcast
stitches to attach the beret, head, arms,
and legs. Sew the beret onto the back of
the head, and attach the eyes and mouth.
Sew the head, arms, and legs onto the
body. Pass the thread through the girl's
head to attach the braids.

How to Crochet (refer to Color Table)
Head (single crochet)

Row	Stitches		Color Group
1st row	8 stitches	❦x8	A
2nd row	16 stitches	❦x8	A
3rd row	24 stitches	(❦x1 + ❦x1) x8	A
4th row	32 stitches	(❦x2 + ❦x1) x8	A
5th row	40 stitches	(❦x3 + ❦x1) x8	A
6th row	40 stitches	❦x40	A
7th row	40 stitches	❦x40	B
8th row	40 stitches	❦x40	B
9th row	32 stitches	(❦x1 + ❦x3) x8	B
10th row	24 stitches	(❦x1 + ❦x2) x8	B
11th row	21 stitches	(❦x1 + ❦x6) x3 ●–	B

How to Crochet
Body (single crochet for doll #1, single crochet stripes for doll #2)

Row	Stitches		Color Group
1st row	8 stitches	❦x8	C
2nd row	16 stitches	❦x8	C
3rd row	24 stitches	(❦x1 + ❦x1) x8	C
4th row	24 stitches	❦x24	C
5th row	24 stitches	❦x24	1-C, 2-D
6th row	24 stitches	❦x24	1-C, 2-E
7th row	24 stitches	❦x24	1-D, 2-D
8th row	24 stitches	❦x24	1-D, 2-F
9th row	21 stitches	(❦x1 + ❦x6) x3	1-D, 2-D
10th row	21 stitches	❦x21	1-D, 2-E
11th row	18 stitches	(❦x1 + ❦x5) x3	1-D, 2-D
12th row	15 stitches	(❦x1 + ❦x4) x3	1-D, 2-F
13th row	12 stitches	(❦x1 + ❦x3) x3 ●–	1-D, 2-D

Color Table

	Doll 1	Doll 2
Color Group A (head, legs, tips of arms)	Light brown	Light brown
Color Group B (hair, feet)	Red	Navy blue
Color Group C (main body, legs)	Plain	Sky blue
Color Group D (main body, arms, skirt)	Moss green	Plain
Color Group E (main body, feet, arms, beret)	Navy blue	Yellow green
Color Group F (main body, arms)		Yellow

How to Crochet

Arms (single crochet for doll #1, single crochet stripes for doll #2), 2 pieces

		Color Group 1	Color Group 2
1st row	5 stitches ⬦x5	A	A
2nd row	10 stitches ⬦x5	A	A
3rd row	10 stitches ⬦x10	A	A
4th row	7 stitches (⋏x1 + ⬦x1) x3 + ⬦x1	A	A
5th row	7 stitches ⬦x7	D	D
6th row	7 stitches ⬦x7	D	E
7th row	7 stitches ⬦x7	D	D
8th row	7 stitches ⬦x7	D	F
9th row	7 stitches ⬦x7	D	D
10th row	7 stitches ⬦x7	D	E
11th row	7 stitches ⬦x7	D	D
12th row	7 stitches ⬦x7	D	F
13th row	7 stitches ⬦x7 ●	D	D

Make a turning chain to sew the arms of doll #2.

Legs (single crochet), 2 pieces

		Color Group 1	Color Group 2
1st row	7 stitches ⬦x7	E	B
2nd row	14 stitches ⬦x7	E	B
3rd row	14 stitches ⬦x14	E	B
4th row	13 stitches ⬦x12 + ⋏x1	E	B
→ 5th row	9 stitches ⋏x1 + ⬦x7 + ⋏x1 Leave 2 stitches.	E	B
← 6th row	7 stitches ⋏x1 + ⬦x5 + ⋏x1	E	B
→ 7th row	5 stitches ⋏x1 + ⬦x3 + ⋏x1	E	B
← 8th row	3 stitches ⋏x1 + ⬦x1 + ⋏x1	E	B
9th row	12 stitches ⬦x12 Pick up the stitches.	C	C
10th row	11 stitches ⋏x1 + ⬦x10	C	C
11th–13th rows	11 stitches ⬦x11	A	C
14th row	10 stitches ⋏x1 + ⬦x9	A	C
15th row	10 stitches ⬦x10 ●	A	C

Work on the 1st–4th rows in a crochet flat pattern to make the heel, then crochet the 9th row by picking up the stitches from the 5th–8th rows to stitch the heel and instep. (Refer to page 59.)

How to Crochet
Ornament for beret (single crochet)—Color Group E

⬦⬦⬦ 1 row

How to Crochet

Beret (single crochet)—Color Group E

1st row	8 stitches ⬦x8
2nd row	16 stitches ⬦x8
3rd row	24 stitches (⬦x1 + ⬦x5) x2
4th row	24 stitches ⬦x24
5th row	21 stitches (⋏x1 + ⬦x6) x3 ●

Skirt (single crochet)—Color Group D

1st row	36 stitches (⬦x1 + ⬦x1) x12
2nd row	36 stitches ⬦x36
3rd row	42 stitches (⬦x5 + ⬦x1) x6
4th row	42 stitches ⬦x42 ●

Pick up the stitches of the 7th row of the body to knit the skirt.

Assembling the Body Parts (refer to page 51)

Attach the eyes

Overcast stitches

Chain stitches with red thread

2.4 in (6 cm)

Take 9.1 inches (23 cm) of 3 strands of red yarn and pass them through the 7th row. Work on the 6 strands of yarn altogether to make braids

4 stitches

1 row

14.2 in (36 cm)

Flatten the joint sides and sew them using overcast stitches

Stuff less cotton in the sleeves and none around the joint parts of the legs

3 rows from the starting point

3 rows from the starting point of body

Attach an ornament to the starting point of the beret

Beret

Overcast stitches

Head

Flatten the joint sides and sew them using overcast stitches

Back

The boy is sewn in the same way as the girl except for the hair and skirt

● White Seal

See pages 46–47 for photos.
• •

Yarns
Seal: Medium fur type, 35 oz (90 g)
White
Scarf: Heavy type, 3.2 oz (8 g)
Blue and pink

Tools
Size #4 (3.5 mm) and size #8 (5 mm)
  crochet hooks
Tapestry needle

Other materials
1 pair of sky blue washer beads for
0.7 in (1.8 cm) eyes
Synthetic cotton
Black rubber band
Small pieces of black and red felt

Tips
Pick up a single strand of yarn. Using a
size #8 (5 mm) crochet hook, start the seal
from a foundation ring with only single
crochet stitches. Leave a long tail at the
end and fasten off. Stuff cotton into every
body part. Attach the nose tip, black dots,
and whiskers on the nose. Use overcast
stitches to attach the nose, arms, and
legs. Sew the nose onto the head, and
attach the eyes and tongue. Sew the arms
and legs onto the body. Using a size #4
(3.5 mm) crochet hook, crochet the scarf
and roll it around the neck.

How to Crochet (refer to Color Table)
Head (single crochet)

1st row	7 stitches	♀x7
2nd row	14 stitches	♀♀x7
3rd row	21 stitches	(♀x1 + ♀♀x1) x7
4th row	28 stitches	(♀x2 + ♀♀x1) x7
5th row	35 stitches	(♀x3 + ♀♀x1) x7
6th row	42 stitches	(♀x4 + ♀♀x1) x7
7th row	49 stitches	(♀x5 + ♀♀x1) x7
8th–10th rows	49 stitches	♀x49
11th row	42 stitches	(♙x1 + ♀x5) x7
12th row	35 stitches	(♙x1 + ♀x4) x7
13th row	28 stitches	(♙x1 + ♀x3) x7
14th row	21 stitches	(♙x1 + ♀x2) x7 ●━

How to Crochet
Arms (single crochet), 2 pieces

1st row	7 stitches	♀x7
2nd row	7 stitches	♀x7
3rd row	7 stitches	♀x7
4th row	14 stitches	♀♀x7
5th row	14 stitches	♀♀x3 + ♀x2 + ♙x3 + ♀x3
6th row	14 stitches	♀x14
7th row	14 stitches	♀x14
8th row	16 stitches	♀x2 + ♀♀x2 + ♀x10
9th row	16 stitches	♀x16 ●━

Legs (single crochet), 2 pieces

1st row	7 stitches	♀x7
2nd row	7 stitches	♀x7
3rd row	7 stitches	♀x7
4th row	14 stitches	♀♀x7
5th row	14 stitches	♀♀x3 + ♀x2 + ♙x3 + ♀x3
6th row	14 stitches	♀x14 ●━

How to Crochet
Body (single crochet)

1st row	7 stitches	♦x7
2nd row	7 stitches	♦x7
3rd row	7 stitches	♦x7
4th row	14 stitches	♣x7
5th row	14 stitches	♦x14
6th row	14 stitches	♦x14
7th row	21 stitches	(♦x1 + ♣x1) x7
8th row	21 stitches	♦x21
← 9th row	28 stitches	(♦x2 + ♣x1) x7
→ 10th row	18 stitches	Change directions ♦x18 and leave 10 stitches
← 11th row	18 stitches	Change directions ♦x18
← 12th row	28 stitches	Pick up the 10 stitches left behind. ♦x28
→ 13th row	18 stitches	Change directions ♦x18 and leave 10 stitches
← 14th row	18 stitches	Change directions ♦x18
← 15th row	28 stitches	Pick up the 10 stitches left behind. ♦x28
→ 16th row	18 stitches	Change directions ♦x18 and leave 10 stitches
← 17th row	18 stitches	Change directions ♦x18
← 18th row	28 stitches	Pick up the 10 stitches left behind. ♦x28
→ 19th row	18 stitches	Change directions ♦x18 and leave 10 stitches
← 20th row	18 stitches	Change directions ♦x18
21th row	28 stitches	Pick up the 10 stitches left behind ♦x28
22nd row	35 stitches	(♦x3 + ♣x3) x7
23rd row	35 stitches	♦x35
24th row	35 stitches	♦x35
25th row	28 stitches	(♠x3 + ♦x1) x7
26th row	28 stitches	♦x28
27th row	28 stitches	♦x28
28th row	21 stitches	(♠x2 + ♦x1) x7 •—

How to Crochet
Nose (single crochet), 2 pieces

1st row	7 stitches	♦x7
2nd row	14 stitches	♣x7
3rd row	14 stitches	♦x14
4th row	7 stitches	♠x7 •—

Nose tip (single crochet)

1st Row	8 stitches	♦x8 •—

How to Crochet
Scarf (single crochet)

1st –100th rows   5 stitches
Change colors for every 5 rows

Actual size patterns for the black dots and tongue.

Black felt

Insert this part under the cheeks

Red felt

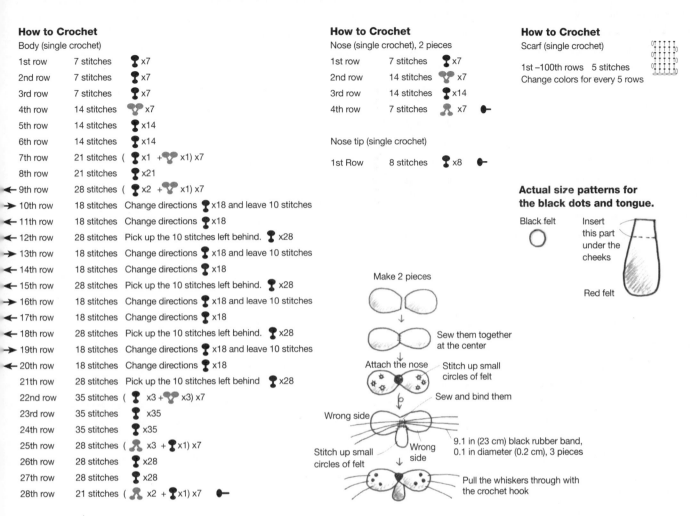

Make 2 pieces

Sew them together at the center

Attach the nose
Stitch up small circles of felt
Sew and bind them

Wrong side
9.1 in (23 cm) black rubber band, 0.1 in diameter (0.2 cm), 3 pieces

Stitch up small circles of felt
Wrong side

Pull the whiskers through with the crochet hook

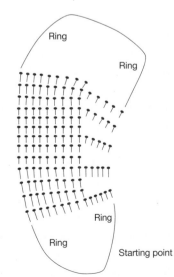

Ring
Ring
Ring
Ring
Starting point

Assembling the Body Parts (refer to page 51)

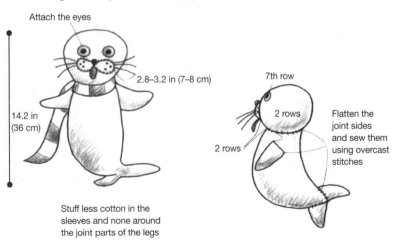

Attach the eyes
2.8–3.2 in (7–8 cm)
14.2 in (36 cm)
Stuff less cotton in the sleeves and none around the joint parts of the legs

7th row
2 rows
2 rows
Flatten the joint sides and sew them using overcast stitches

About the Author

Tomoko Takamori
As a researcher of knitting and crochet, Tomoko Takamori started her career in amigurumi creation in 1993. Her excellent, colorful, and artistic works have attracted many admirers. She has published several books on crocheting, such as *Book of Amigurumi*. Recently, she devotes her time to introducing small and practical items that can be knitted easily.